The True Measure of a Woman

You are more than what you see

The True Measure of a Woman

*You are more than
what you see*

LISA BEVERE

CREATION
HOUSE
Orlando, FL

THE TRUE MEASURE OF A WOMAN by Lisa Bevere
Published by Creation House
Strang Communications Company
600 Rinehart Road, Lake Mary, Florida 32746
Web site: http://www.creationhouse.com

Unless otherwise noted, all Scripture quotations are from the Holy
Bible, New International Version. Copyright © 1973, 1978, 1984,
International Bible Society. Used by permission.

Scripture quotations marked NKJV are from the New King James
Version of the Bible. Copyright © 1979, 1980, 1982 by Thomas
Nelson Inc., publishers. Used by permission.

Scripture quotations marked AMP are from the Amplified Bible.
Old Testament copyright © 1965, 1987 by the Zondervan
Corporation. The Amplified New Testament copyright © 1954,
1958, 1987 by the Lockman Foundation. Used by permission.

Library of Congress Cataloging-in-Publication Data:
Bevere, Lisa.
     The true measure of a woman / Lisa Bevere.
          p.   cm.
     ISBN: 0-88419-487-6 (pbk.)
     1. Woman (Christian theology) 2. Self-perception—
Religious aspects—Christianity. 3. Self-evaluation. 4. Self-esteem—
Religious aspects—Christianity. 5. Bevere, Lisa. I. Title.
BT704.B48 1997
248.8'43—dc21   97-31174
                                                                  CIP

78901234 BBG 87654321
Printed in the United States of America

Acknowledgments

My most sincere appreciation to Tom Freiling at Creation House. You believed that there was a book in me, and encouraged me to write more than you'll ever know.

To the entire Creation House staff: Thanks for all your support. Alyse, you did nothing but improve this book. Steve and Joy, thanks for standing with John and I to see that these books come forth and into the hands of others.

To my mother: You have been a source of encouragement, strength, and inspiration.

To my four precious sons—

Addison, I'll always love you the longest; I am proud of the boy you are and the man you will be one day. You are tender and brave, honest and bright.

Austin, you are my "lion bunny;" strong yet sensitive. I love your creativity and sense of justice.

Alexander, you are my "joy boy;" you are growing up sweet and strong.

Arden, you are a child filled with fire and determination, yet tempered by a submissive heart.

I love you each more than words can express.

My deepest love and appreciation to my husband, friend, and colaborer. John, may we never be satisfied until we see His glory revealed.

To my Father God: You know that I did not write this book, but that it was breathed by Your Spirit. Thank You for this honor. I give You all the glory. I am eternally grateful.

This Book Belongs To
'qenia L. Garnett
Burnside Road

Contents

Foreword

by

John Bevere

W HAT IS your value? What is your worth? This answer should be established in every human's heart and mind. Everything in this earth is assigned a value. We would not pay two hundred thousand dollars for a house that was only worth fifty thousand. If we did, it would not only be an unprofitable purchase . . . but a loss.

Jesus posed this question: "For what profit is it to a man if he gains the whole world, and loses his own soul?" (Matt. 16:26, NKJV). The question reveals the truth that if we gave ourselves in exchange for all the wealth, power, influence, and wisdom of this world, it would result in an unprofitable loss. Think of it: If we exchanged what we are worth to own every business, all the gold, all the money, and all the riches this earth possesses, it would be an unprofitable exchange. There are many who would give far less to own such earthly wealth.

So what is your value? John 3:16, (NKJV) says, "For God so loved the world that He gave His only begotten Son . . ." God gave Jesus in exchange for you. "For you know that God paid a ransom to save you from the empty life you inherited from your ancestors. And the ransom he paid was not mere gold or silver. He paid for you with the precious lifeblood of Christ" (1 Pet. 1:18–19, NLT). If you had been the only person on earth, Jesus still would have died for you! God never makes unprofitable deals, just as you would not knowingly pay a greater price than the actual worth of an item. In God's eyes, you alone are worth the measure of the life of His Son!

Many believers mentally acknowledge this truth without ever being established in it. This book contains powerful teaching and illustrations which bring this truth to light. After reading only half of the manuscript, I approached my wife and expressed my disappointment with just one thing. Concerned, she asked, "What is that?" I replied, "The title of your book won't draw men to read it."

The True Measure of a Woman contains some of the most profound revelation from God's Word that I have ever read. It is revealing. It is motivating. It is life-changing. I can honestly say that what you are about to read is from the heart of God! Read this book with an open heart and you will not be the same. I want to ask every one of you to do something: When your life has been changed after reading this book, please give a copy of it to a man and tell him to read every word! If he looks at you a bit funny, tell him, "John Bevere says every man ought to read this book!"

I have had the privilege of being married to Lisa for almost fifteen years. Her life is one of godliness and virtue. I trust her with my life, and so can you. God has entrusted her with a message for His people. You have not received this book by chance; it is a divine appointment. May God greatly enrich you as you read!

Introduction

GOD DELIGHTS in taking the arena of our greatest fear and putting us in position to face it. This is how He trains our hands for war and our fingers for battle. In 1982 God commissioned me to minister to women. At the time I just wept, "Not women, God! Anyone but women! I'll go anywhere, but don't make me stand before women!"

I had no heart for women; most of the time they just annoyed me. I didn't trust them. I felt more comfortable with the guys. At least *guys said what they meant* and *meant what they said.* Women, on the other hand, seemed to speak a very vague and precarious language, one that I could never seem to master.

It seemed that I was always saying the wrong thing.

I brought this concern to a precious man who had adopted me as his spiritual daughter. I shared what God had placed before me. "I'm not like them," I lamented. "They are all so sweet and smile, saying 'Praise the Lord!' all the time—and then . . ."

"They stab you in the back?" he interjected.

"Well, not *all* of them," I stammered. "I just don't fit in. I think there is something wrong with me." Tears welled in my eyes as I looked down.

This precious man took my hand, looked me in the eyes, and said something that set me free. "Lisa, you're not *supposed* to fit in. God made you the way you are. Don't try to be like everyone else." He continued, "Women all over are hurting. That is why they hurt others. You need to ask God to give you His heart for women. Often that will come through your own personal pain."

How true his words have proven to be! This book is my heart. It is a book for every one of you who have ever felt like you just do not fit in. It's for those of you who have felt that you are on the outside looking in, wishing there was more than what you've seen. This is not merely a women's issues book; it's about heart issues. God is calling us to be more than we've ever been—more than we have ever envisioned that we could become.

At the very onset of this book, I want to challenge you to read it differently than you read other books. I want you to *participate* with this book, not just read it in quiet thought. I want you to dare to address the issues raised within these pages on a very real and tangible level. I want the truths in this book to become woven into the fabric of your life. The only way for this to happen is for you to apply these truths personally.

This is easier said than done. It is always easier to remove yourself emotionally from a book and just process its contents mentally, while remaining very detached. But this is not where change is forged. It is the truth we *live*, not the truth we *know*, that sets us free. In order to find such truth, we must *be honest* with ourselves, *answer* some questions, and then *change* the way we have looked at things.

The degree to which you are honest, open, and transparent is the degree to which you will allow the light of God's Word to penetrate. Only God's Word can separate the precious from the vile.

To accomplish this, I invite you to keep a journal or notepad handy as you go through this book. There will be questions only you can answer, and it is important that you record these answers as you go. These questions may also bring to light questions of your own, ones that you will want to write down so you can bring them before the Father later, during times of prayer.

Because I am asking something of you, accountability becomes a factor. It is quite possible that you may want to work through this book as a Bible study for a group, or separately during your personal devotion time. Choose whichever way you will best commit to using this book in your search. Make the establishment of God's truth a priority in your life. I invite you to travel on with me to the paths of truth.

—LISA BEVERE
ORLANDO, FLORIDA

*God awakens an inquisitive
questioning in us when He wants us to go
searching for answers.*

1

Asking Questions

"I praise you because I am fearfully and wonderfully made."
—*Psalm 139:14a*

T HIS BOOK is the culmination of my ongoing search for answers to a series of questions that I have wrestled with since my teen years. They are questions I believe every woman—no matter her walk in life or experience—mulls over as the different seasons of her life ebb and flow. These are simple questions really—questions like, "How do I fit in or relate to the world around me?" and "What is the measure of my worth?"

While I believed I knew the answers to such questions, not too long ago I had the opportunity to view them in a new and different light. It was an unexpected moment when I knew my outlook would be altered permanently.

I had escaped the noise and clamor of a house filled with four young sons to enjoy the quiet of my husband's office after hours. It was the place I had chosen to conduct a radio interview for my book, *Out of Control and Loving It*. Although its title conveyed an image of high energy and lots of activity, I knew the radio listeners would still appreciate a quiet background while I discussed the book. Radio is wonderful and relaxed because no can see you. So, clad in baseball cap and a warm-up suit, I waited for my interviewer to call, since the program would be taped via phone to air later.

A few weeks earlier I had spoken with Sarah, my interviewer, to schedule the show and get acquainted. She was pleasant and professional. She was honest to let me know that she had yet to read my book, and that she would probably only have time to scan it before we spoke again. Sarah explained that she received so many books to review that she rarely read them all the way through prior to interviewing the authors. She suggested that I come up with some questions and arrive at some idea of what I wanted to discuss. She said she would call a few minutes early so we could go over my questions before the interview.

So there I was, in the stillness of my husband's empty office, flipping through my book and making notes for myself in the margins and folding down the corners of pages that contained points of interest. As I did this, I prayed that those who needed to hear this interview would be drawn to listen and that most of all, it would glorify God. I waited, a little nervous, never suspecting the impact the interview would have on me.

The phone broke the silence and startled me. It was Sarah, but this time she sounded excited: "I don't want to talk now and diminish your answers on the air, but I have *read* your book! And we need to address some things. I have my questions ready. I want to highlight your *gossip chapter* in our interview!"

The gossip chapter! I hadn't marked anything from that chapter! Sarah's enthusiasm had caught me totally off guard. I had planned to talk about the anger chapter. Frantically I flipped pages, dog-earring some of them and hastily attaching sticky notes. I took a deep breath and reminded myself of the question my husband always poses whenever he sees me spinning off into such flurries of panic just before an interview: "Didn't *you* write the book?" The truth was *I had,* and the gossip chapter was especially personal!

For the next hour Sarah and I discussed the tendency of women to gossip and the various ulterior motives behind it—namely . . . fear. Sarah had blown asunder any facade of professionalism when she opened the program with a candid and broken confession of her own tendency to gossip. She pleaded with the unseen radio audience to be open and transformed in this area of their own personal lives. She confessed how, in her profession, she had always considered gossip to be "networking."

The questions Sarah asked probed deeper than those of an unbiased interviewer. They echoed the cries and excitement of a searching heart that had suddenly found truth. Together we shared, pleaded, and prayed with our audience. When the interview was over, we continued to talk. Sarah opened up even more with me, and we ended by praying together. As I hung up the phone, I felt as though I had just said good-bye to a college roommate. For a moment I sat alone, acutely aware that something different had transpired.

HEARING HEART-TO-HEART

ALTHOUGH I HAD never seen her, I felt I knew this woman more intimately than most of the women I meet in person. I did not know whether she was young or old, rich or poor, fat or thin, black or white, blonde, brunette, or redhead. There had been no way to read her facial expressions and body language as we talked. I couldn't take note of whether she was dressed for success or dressed for comfort. Yet I felt I knew her.

Then it dawned on me that this bond might not have been made if we had met in person. We may have done that unconscious check-out of each other, and we may have been influenced by each other's visual impressions. Though I could never pick her out of a crowd, I felt I knew this woman called Sarah more than some of my own neighbors. I had not *seen* her, but I had *heard* her—not the fake her, the *real* her. I had heard something I could never look upon, because I had heard her heart.

Seizing the moment, the Holy Spirit arrested my racing thoughts and said, *"That is how I know you."* He whispered, "I cannot see you, for you are hidden in Christ. I can only hear you. It is your spoken words and the unbroken communication of your heart that I listen to."

That was right! Because I had no righteousness of my own, the righteousness of Jesus had been appropriated to me in redemption. God could not look upon me, so I was covered in the sin offering of Jesus the Christ. Not unlike a radio interview, it didn't matter to the Holy Spirit what I looked like; it only mattered what I said. Of course, the Holy Spirit had another frequency— one that even the strongest satellite couldn't monitor. It was the frequency of the silent communication of my heart!

That's good—and that's bad! Good, because unlike us, God neither judges nor is affected by what He sees . . . and bad, because I tend to be more aware of what I see than what I do not see. This means I often unconsciously measure myself by parameters God does not even use! It's bad, because though I had really grown in certain spiritual dimensions—my confession, for instance—I still had not conquered the vivid and violent battleground of my thoughts.

That night my husband and I went out on a much-needed dinner date. Over our meal I shared with him what had happened during the radio interview that afternoon. I explained to John how women tend to look at things. I used different scenarios to illustrate the tendency toward competition and the measuring of each other by what we see or perceive. I confessed my tendency to do this and explained how frustrated I was when I knew I was being reduced to what I looked like or wore. Surely I was not alone in my frustration. My spirit sensed such an urgency for truth. I was tired of hearing the pat excuses I had always so readily accepted: "You know *women;* that is just the way they are!" or, "It's a *woman thing!*" Such statements may sound true, but they are not the truth!

I wanted God's truth, not excuses, not even for myself. This would mean peeling away some layers, like the dry and dirty outer skin of an onion—layer after layer of misconceptions and bad information until I found some pure truth.

QUESTIONS AND ANSWERS

GOD AWAKENS an inquisitive questioning in us when He wants us to go searching for answers. To learn, we must first ask questions. Questions are not always comfortable. Remember school, when you had a question and you were afraid you would sound stupid if you asked it? Or when the teacher asked you a question and you were unsure of the answer?

Well, here is our question, the one we will repeatedly ask in the pages of this book: *What is the true measure of a woman?*

You could poll any mixed group of people and receive a variety of answers. Each answer would be spawned by variances in culture, gender, and age. Ask a preschooler, and the standard of a woman is bound to be their mother. To an older child, the measure would broaden to include teachers, athletes, or performers. To a young adult or teenager, a woman is measured in comparison with the images projected by models, Hollywood personalities, and the cultural influences of their age group. How a woman looks. What she wears. Now the physical and sexual differences are pronounced and overshadow the innocence of a child's former perceptions of a woman.

If we are more selective and question only a certain group of women, we'll receive yet another sampling of answers. Personal and vulnerable answers, the ones you only get when men are not around.

But I don't believe we will find the answer we are searching for in any of these public polls or personal opinions. Nor can it be drawn from my experiences or those of others; these are too limited. Our culture cannot answer us. It is tormented with too many questions of its own, questions it cannot answer because of inconsistency and the prevalent influence of the spirit of this world. We could ask our mothers, but like us, most of them are still searching.

Right now I am not addressing any particular group with this question. Although I am not conducting an official opinion poll, I am going to question you—even knowing that I may never hear your answer. The written word has the power to probe directly into the secret place of your silent thoughts. You cannot hear my voice, and I cannot hear your answer. Through the pages of this book, you and I can communicate on a more intimate, unspoken level, one that would not be possible even if we were face-to-face.

You may have already toyed with what your reply will be. Now I will ask you directly, and I want you to stop and write your answer down in the space provided:

❦

What is the true measure of a woman? Her character: the way she treats others, how she conducts herself, her kindness, willingness of spirit

You may be thinking, "Hey, if I had the answer, I wouldn't be reading this book!" Please remember what we covered in the introduction. (If you didn't read it, please go back.) This is a participation—not an observation—book. To learn, we must not merely see but truly understand what we already know. It is imperative that you and I interact, although at this point you may find this awkward or difficult. You may find this question hard to answer specifically. That's all right; be vague. And if you have no idea, write down, "I have no idea!" Above all, be honest. This is not a test, and your answer will not be graded. No one will even see your answer unless you choose to show them. This book is simply a search for truth.

I don't presume to know all life's answers, but this book is from my heart to yours and I believe it bears a glimpse of our Father's heart too. Through its quiet pages, we will talk—and it is my prayer that the power of the Holy Spirit will overshadow all we discuss so that together we may glean His wisdom.

I challenge you to join me in this search for the true measure of a woman; you must already be curious. As you turn these page and read the truth of God, it will remove the scales that kept you from seeing. Let His light illuminate your eyes.

Pray with me:

> *Father God, reveal Your truth to me by Your Word and Spirit. Lord, give me eyes to see, ears to hear, and a heart that perceives and understands. Above all these, Lord, grant me a willing and pliable heart that will believe and apply Your truth so that it may bring forth Your fruit in my life. I give You permission to change my perspective. Reveal Yourself, for You are the way, the truth, and the life. Amen.*

Believe that He will.

We need

to totally change

how we look at things in

order to perceive God's

will.

2

Cleaning Closets

Do not conform any longer to the pattern of this world, but be transformed by the renewing of your mind. Then you will be able to test and approve what God's will is—his good, pleasing and perfect will.

—ROMANS 12:2

D ID YOU write down an answer? As we dig deeper your answer may change or broaden, but don't go back and change your original response. Your initial response (even if it was, "I honestly don't know!") will serve as a gauge by which you can measure how much you have learned or changed. It will give you a perspective from which to work. When we have teachable hearts, we should not fear where we have been because it is an integral part of where we are going. At this early stage, our answers serve merely as assessments of where we are.

Right now, there is no wrong or right answer. We can always be learning and therefore remain forever teachable. I am always so impressed by older, wiser women who are still capable of learning from others. I watch them and think, *That's how I want to be!* It was only when I was very young and knew nothing that I despised all but the counsel of my peers.

In our search, we will ask more questions and answer them too. Your responses may surprise you. You may even have the opportunity to answer, "I don't know"—which hopefully will awaken a desire deep within to pursue truth.

CLEARING OUT THE CLUTTER

OUR SEARCH for truth could be compared to cleaning out a bedroom closet. I usually only tackle cleaning out my closet when I absolutely have to. It is only when I find clutter and disorder so intimidating that I can stand it no longer that I finally resolve to clean my closet. A variety of circumstances will inspire my rampage to clean and organize. It may be that I see someone in need of something that I know hangs unused in my closet. Or perhaps a move will necessitate such a cleaning jag. My need to clean may simply arise in retaliation after innocently walking in to pull a sweater off the shelf—and the whole stack leaps out, toppling sweaters onto my head and then onto the floor. Now a challenge has gone forth to clean out that closet—or else—and I pick up the gauntlet, determined to set all things in order.

I counterattack, grabbing fallen clothes and everything else from the shelves and hanging rods. These items are rapidly transported into the light and tumbled onto the master bed, with the overflow portioned to the living-room sofa. With everything out, I vacuum the closet floor and pick up the stray dry cleaning tags, safety pins, and pocket change as I work. Now my closet seems much bigger and far less intimidating. Now I'm ready to reorganize and rehang. I go over each item before hanging it up or granting it shelf space. I ask an assortment of questions. *Do I still need this maternity dress if I'm not planning any more children?* My mind argues, *That's what you thought two children ago!* But I fight back, *No! I'll give it away.*

Then I make some observations. "Oh no, *this* was hung up dirty!" . . . "I stained this the first time I wore it" . . . "I paid too much to just throw it away" . . . "Maybe a new cleaning product will come out that removes three-year-old stains." "No! Lisa, just *throw it away!*"

I find there is just no room for that heavy winter outfit in my July closet. So I put it in off-season storage. After discarding the prolific hangers that seem to have multiplied since my last closet purge, I discover there is space to hang more clothes when all the empty coathangers are cleared out. With all the unnecessary and inappropriate items removed, I now have room for the important things—the things I can use.

This whole process has provided a moment of truth for me. I can often gauge my spiritual well-being by seeing what I fight to hang on to.

Other times it is exciting because I find things that I thought were lost, or rediscover items I forgot I had. When I know I have misplaced something, I am a little apprehensive as I sort through pockets, purses, and piles, fearful of what I may *not* find. Before the clutter was removed I could never be certain if the missing item lurked somewhere in the dark recesses of my closet. If after clearing everything out I announce to my husband that I still can't find that item, even he will join me in my search. (Until that moment his answer was, "You'll find it when you clean out your closet.")

TACKLING THE TOUGH ISSUES

IN THIS BOOK, we are going to tackle the closets of our minds. It is so much easier when you don't have to face it alone. I'm going to help you with this process. I will face it *with you.* There are many outfits (past experiences) and accessories (thought processes) that you should never wear again. They are dated and no longer fit and rob space from what you should be wearing right now. Some items should be thrown away. Others should be given to those who could really use them.

Go ahead: Examine the contents of your closet. Is it from long ago and you kept it, for safety, just in case it came back in style? Was it trendy then but now is it out of date? (Remember, fashion and events never repeat themselves in quite the same way . . . so pitch it!) Has it outlived its usefulness to you (like my maternity clothes) but could be passed on to bless another? (Passing things on to the next generation keeps them fresh and alive; retaining them means they get musty and old.)

Pass on the faithfulness of God and His provision in your life and share it with others. As we share these "outfits" of our testimony with others, we help those who are yet struggling with areas we have since overcome. Sharing in this manner renews our own faith, because we are encouraged to believe that God will be faithful once again.

Some items are soiled with guilt and must be washed in the Word of God before they can be worn again. Others bear stains that can't be removed; don't mourn their loss—just throw them away. They represent the various disappointments and failures in the past, things we need to forgive and forget. In this closet we will find things we thought were lost. We'll come to the realization that some items cannot be found in the confines of our closet.

Cleaning closets is comparable to the process of renewing our minds.

> Do not conform any longer to the pattern of this world, but be transformed by the renewing of your mind. Then you will be able to test and approve what God's will is—his good, pleasing and perfect will.
>
> —ROMANS 12:2

We want to weigh out, agree with, and apply God's truth in our lives. This requires nothing short of a transformation in our minds. We need to totally change how we look at things in order to to perceive God's will. We cannot determine His plan through the clutter of the counsel of man and the plans of this world. We may rest assured of three characteristics of God's plan for us:

1. It is for good.

2. It is pleasing to Him.

3. It is perfect.

And it is never inappropriate, though at first it may seem uncomfortable. God is ultimately more concerned with our *condition* than our *comfort*. This means there will be times of temporary discomfort in order to bring about eternal comfort. What He provides is drawn from timeless wisdom, and always in good taste. It is flawless, void of stains, rips, and imperfections. God wants to outfit our mind with a whole new outlook.

Just like our closets, our minds can become cluttered by the patterns or trends of this world. These outfits, or thought processes, may look like they belong in our closets the first few years they take up residence. But with the passage of time, they soon appear threadbare and out of sorts. They fit too tight or too loose, too long or too short. Unless our closets—minds—are cleared out and reorganized on a timely and regular basis, we will not be able to test and apply God's truth to our lives.

The standard for determining what remains in our minds and on the rack always must be God's Word. Since the objective of this book is to locate and apply truth, as unpleasant as it may initially be, we are going to need to clean some closets. Left to themselves, our minds will accumulate clutter. And clutter needs to be either stored, refreshed, or removed. If we don't clear out the clutter, we will lack the necessary space for the wisdom and fresh insights that God longs to provide for us.

AS LITTLE CHILDREN

OFTEN WHEN I pick up my children from school they will tumble into the car and excitedly share some new tidbit of knowledge they have gleaned that day. It begins with a challenge, "Mom, did you know . . . ?" Often I will already have this knowledge stored somewhere in the deep recesses of my memory, but in response to my children's excitement—and because I want to hear their unique perspectives—I'll answer, "Tell me!" Then their high-pitched voices will take on a lower, slower, more serious, almost scholarly tone as they explain from their new and fresh view a science, math, or history fact.

Their zeal usually reawakens my awareness of this information, along with the memory of when I learned such facts. When the boys finish their discourse, they almost always conclude with their original question: "Did you know that, Mom?"

I'll answer truthfully, "I did—but I had forgotten that I knew it, because I haven't used that information for so long." My answer always puzzles them. At their age, almost everything they learn is still actively retained because they apply their present knowledge to gather more. Consequently, their mental "closets" are revolving storehouses of actively used "clothes."

Jesus admonishes us to approach the kingdom of God as little children. (See Matthew 18:3.)

This is not a call to immature or childish behavior, but to become childlike. One such childlike attribute is to be inquisitive. My children sometimes exhaust me with their many questions, but a child who does not ask questions is a child who has stopped learning. And a child who is not questioned will not be accurately positioned for learning. That is why children are tested at school each year. It is to see if they can apply what they have mastered.

When my children transferred schools, they were tested for placement to confirm that they had been equipped with the tools necessary to learn in their new environment. When we are childlike, we will maintain an attitude that is forever teachable.

God has created us to respond to our surroundings with excitement, awe, and wonder. This wonder will inspire us to ask questions. I love watching the joy of learning light up the eyes of my two-year-old whenever he discovers something new or masters some new skill. If I just lift him high enough to touch a leaf, he is thrilled and stretches his arms higher yet to embrace the entire branch. To him, every discovery is an adventure, a new tool he can use in his pursuit of understanding the world around him.

As adults, we are to approach life in the same childlike manner. But often our mental closets are too cluttered with outdated information and the cynical outlook of this world. Without our full realization, this clutter colors our perception of everything. To make way for the new, we must rid ourselves of the old. The way we previously looked at things, the standards we have used to measure ourselves in the past, the scale by which we measure others, the limits fear has placed on our lives, the wasteland of our past that has to be left behind. We will address these various forms of clutter individually and in-depth. After all, as a woman I know where you are—though I may not know exactly where you have been.

I don't want to give you the mistaken impression that I am a Pollyanna optimist. I am not. The wonder I experience when I wake up is the shock that it is already morning! Then there is the amazement that my husband is wide awake and happy immediately! I am not. I stumble into the shower just so I can open both eyes. But as my day progresses I begin to see the wonder. The wonder of a baby's skin, the sweetness in my children's eyes, the wonder of the sunlight filtering through the trees outside my breakfast window. The wonder of how messy a kitchen can become after only one meal!

"WHY ME, LORD?"

I AM RIGHT where you are. As a woman, wife, and mother of four boys, I face the same pressures you face. They are often magnified by a husband who travels at least weekly, editing and writing deadlines, and assorted office responsibilities. Add to all this that I also travel and speak.

I have often questioned God's wisdom of choosing me when I already feel totally incapable. One such question-and-answer session happened while I showered (one of the few places I can think undisturbed) in preparation before speaking to a large group of women. I had brought my youngest son who was still nursing and had not slept well in the strange hotel room, where he tossed around all night. At that moment he was at my feet playing in the shower so I could keep an eye on him.

Looking down at him, I asked myself, *What am I doing here? I have already spoken to these women four times over the last three years. I feel as though I have nothing left to say. God, You should get someone professional to do this—not a breast-feeding mother of four!*

I was venting and did not even expect an answer. But, nevertheless, an answer came while I wrestled the tangle of the billowing shower curtain away from my slippery son.

"You are right where they are! Therefore, you will not talk down to them. You'll have compassion on them. Be real and transparent and they will see Me in you."

At that point, I could not even see myself through the steam on the bathroom mirror. I was doubtful, but I felt a peace settle over me.

Later that morning as I entered the crowded sanctuary, I felt the anointing presence of God come upon me. It was very real and tangible, as though someone had come up behind me and draped a cloak about me. It comforted me. My mind again was full of questions as I walked to the platform: *What am I doing here?* My heart knew the answer.

FAR FROM PERFECT

I HAVE attended many women's meetings. Sometimes I knew I was in trouble as soon as the speaker walked up to the pulpit. From what was said and the image projected by the speakers, I got the impression that their lives were perfect, their children were perfect, their marriages were perfect, their finances blessed and abundant.

In comparison, I felt like a failure. Although I *wanted* to be like them, I feared I was too different . . . too imperfect.

I would listen intently to their perfect messages, taking extensive notes. Yet, while my head mentally identified with the principles they taught, my heart did not. I would leave some of these meetings with a list of advice that didn't seem at all applicable to where I was. Their solutions of taking bubblebaths and making more time for myself did not fit in with my busy lifestyle. I left other meetings feeling defeated. If only I read my Bible more often and prayed three hours a day, everything would be perfect! For whatever reason their words seemed to only increase the already heavy yoke I bore. I was simultaneously impressed by these women and intimidated by them.

Over the years I have had one opportunity after another to find out that the lives represented by these speakers and the lives they actually lived varied greatly. They thought that by *acting* perfect, they could honor God and inspire perfection.

Now it was my turn. Would my audience be impressed with me? No, there was no reason for them to be impressed. Instead, I wanted them to feel safe. I wanted them to feel free to let their guard down so that the Word of God could penetrate their hearts. I wanted to disarm them by letting them know I wasn't going to intimidate or hurt them. I had learned that when an audience can identify with the *messenger*, they will more readily identify with the *message*.

I openly shared the Word that God had made flesh in my life. I shared the good, the bad, and the ugly. For it is truly the areas where we have been weak that God will anoint with His strength. Tears streaked their cheeks as I spoke, because it was no longer my voice that they heard, but the Voice within my voice. They recognized in me their own fears and failures. Encouraged by my honesty, they in turn were honest with themselves. I was a mirror that reflected their own fears and struggles. Because they identified with me, they could more easily believe that if God had done it for me then He would certainly do it for them.

At the close of the meeting, these women flooded the altar with tears of joy and repentance. I joined them there as we wept in awe of the sweet and tangible presence of God. We had brought our hearts before Him and He had accepted our offerings.

Courage to Step Out

It is in this same spirit that I write this book. It is not because I think I know it all. *I don't.* I write because I believe with all my heart that it is God's mandate on my life to share the things He has taught me. I write to you because I know you are not so different from me. We face similar struggles, pain, and triumphs. It is not my goal to tell you what to do, but to accompany you on a search. We are sisters, although I have none.

I will share very openly and honestly. Pretense and appearances are void of power and cannot help anyone. Teachings without the practical knowledge of how to apply them do nothing but weigh us down.

Therefore, I commit to hide nothing from you that I feel might help you. You will have the advantage of gleaning from my foolishness, mishaps, and mistakes.

In return, I ask that you dare to do the same. Dare to be open and honest with yourself. What we hide eventually ensnares and imprisons us. It grows strongest in the shadows of shame and condemnation.

The gospel we preach extends beyond the eternal hope we have because Jesus rose from the dead and restored mankind to God. It is a gospel that empowers us as we live here and now, and its truth will invade every area where we allow Christ to impact us and change our lives.

We must summon the courage as individuals and step out from behind the facades where we have hidden ourselves.

Even in the church, some act as though they never really needed a Savior. The truth is, we all have sinned and fallen short. Our closets are cluttered and full.

Some like it that way. They like the feel of all that clutter. They feel safe holding on to the past. They will tell you they don't have room for any more, because their closets are already bursting at the seams, and they will insist that they already know everything they need to know. They are satisfied with what they have.

> He who is full loathes honey, but to the hungry even what
> is bitter tastes sweet.
>
> —PROVERBS 27:7

Cleaning out the misinformation and clutter of the world from our lives may appear bitter. But we will find, as we empty ourselves of what only temporarily satisfies, that we will have an appetite for more. If we remain full, even the honey of God's wisdom will seem unappetizing. Just like a second round of dessert after you have already eaten a Thanksgiving banquet, what looked so good at the beginning of the meal now causes you to groan in discomfort just looking at it.

I believe you are hungry and that is why you are giving the gift of your time in order to read this book. I believe you want more than what you've had, and are therefore willing to give more of yourself to God.

So here are a few more questions for you to answer. Again, bear in mind that this is not a test. I am going to ask these questions asking in the figurative terms of closet-cleaning, but it is the heart's storage that we are actually dealing with. These questions are simply so we can locate where your heart is, and the answers can be written in the space provided. Or for more privacy, your answers can be recorded on a separate piece of paper or inside a journal:

Are you intimidated by the thought of cleaning out the closet of your mind? _____

Even so, are you ready to do it? _____

(I made the first two simple *yes/no* questions so you could prove to yourself you could do it!)

What are some things you think you might find inside your closet that need to be thrown away? Please be specific. List any stained items from your past that need to be discarded. _____

_____

_____

_____

_____

What are some valuable articles that you need to pass on? Remember those maternity clothes. Recount God's proven faithfulness. _____

_____

_____

_____

Whom would you like to share these items with? _____

_____

_____

_____

Are there items that need to be laundered in God's forgiveness? _____

_____

_____

_____

Are you ashamed of the clutter in your closet? _____

_____

Are you ready to make room for the new by tossing out the old? _____

_____

We can only

rightly divide truth

when we have first applied it

to our own hearts.

3

Honest Measures

Do not judge, or you too will be judged. For in the same way you judge others, you will be judged, and with the measure you use, it will be measured to you.

—*MATTHEW 7:1–2*

HONESTY AND TRUTH will always outlive lies. This world's standards are lies. There are true standards of measurement in God's kingdom. They may not be measured in actual inches or centimeters but definite units of measure nevertheless exist. The incremental size of such units does not matter; God uses units of measure to designate His proportional return to us.

We will see this theme repeated time and again in God's Word. We cannot judge truth until we know and apply truth to ourselves. Without a clear and accurate perspective, we will not recognize the truth when it presents itself. It is imperative that we first remove any obstructions that may bar us from the truth. We are warned:

> Do not judge, or you too will be judged. For in the same way you judge others, you will be judged, and with the measure you use, it will be measured to you.
> —MATTHEW 7:1–2

If we judge, we will be judged. This is a spiritual principle. One day while drying my hair, I was mentally judging a friend who had hurt me. I told myself, *I always knew she was this way. I'm staying away from her!*

This person had repeatedly hurt me. Over the years I had flitted in and out of a friendship with her. One minute we were the best of friends, the next enemies without any apparent cause for the shift in sentiment. Then she would float back into a relationship with me, only to have the cycle play itself out again later. Gossip was inevitably involved, and I decided I was finally through with her!

After making this determination, I expected to feel freedom but instead I felt grieved as the Spirit checked me. I defended my position: "I'm *right* to judge her; she *is* this way!"

GOD, THE ONLY JUDGE

IMMEDIATELY I sensed the Spirit of God question me. "Is that what you want Me to say about *you?*"

I was stunned; after all, *I* wasn't the issue here! What did *I* have to do with this? *I* was talking about *her.* The Holy Spirit continued, "When you judge someone you are saying they are never going to change and therefore you don't have to be reconciled with them. If you judge them, then I must judge you. Do you want me to say, 'Lisa is never going to change?'"

I thought about it. I knew that on the day of judgment God would look at one group and, in essence, say, "Though I've given you a chance time and time again to repent, you never have. You are never going to change. Therefore, there is no reconciliation for you." This group of people would then be told to depart eternally from His presence.

I knew that God would also judge the other group, His sheep, because He knew they would never change either, that they would always love Him and stay faithful to Him. God could see in a dimension unknown to man because He sees into the unseen, unspoken treasuries of our hearts.

> There is only one Lawgiver and Judge, the one who is able to save and destroy. But you—who are you to judge your neighbor?
>
> —JAMES 4:12

I had presumed to know someone else's heart, and when I judged this person I was grieved because I was placing myself under judgment. God alone is judge and He will share this position with no one. I knew this young woman's actions, but I could only guess at her motives.

Although I thought my information was accurate, it was at best incomplete. It is important to note that this conversation never hit the airwaves; it took place only in my head. I never intended to publicly denounce her, but I had pronounced her guilty as prosecutor and judge in the biased court of my heart.

Now that I had seen the truth, I wanted to repent. But I was concerned that my repentance might lead me back into an unhealthy relationship with her. Before praying, I protested, "God, it's true! This cycle keeps happening."

The Holy Spirit gently encouraged me, "I did not say you have to fellowship with her or that your assessment was totally incorrect—only that your reaction to it is wrong."

PARTLY RIGHT, PARTLY WRONG

IT WAS THEN that I realized it is possible to be right *and* wrong. I needed to separate this woman's actions from her motives. It was within reason to decide that her *actions* warranted my caution in all future interactions. I would need to exercise God's wisdom in my relationship with her. But I was not to set myself up as judge over her.

> Because judgment without mercy will be shown to anyone who has not been merciful. Mercy triumphs over judgment!
> —JAMES 2:13

My judgment had been harsh, not allowing for any recourse or repentance on her part. I had forgotten that the measure or amount I had apportioned for her judgment was the same measure, manner, or proportion God would choose when He portioned mine. I have come to this realization—that though I *deserve* judgment, I *need* mercy. If I want mercy, I must therefore be merciful, because only mercy triumphs over judgment.

We receive God's mercy not because we deserve it but because, in Christ, mercy always triumphs!

> Why do you look at the speck of sawdust in your brother's eye and pay no attention to the plank in your own eye? How can you say to your brother, "Let me take the speck out of your eye," when all the time there is a plank in your own eye? You hypocrite, first take the plank out of your own eye, and then you will see clearly to remove the speck from your brother's eye.
> —MATTHEW 7:3–5

I probably had enough planks in my eyes to build an entertainment center. My most prominent plank was a tendency to be critical and to judge, while this woman's speck was a tendency to gossip.

This scripture must be interpreted in context with the preceding scripture—*Do not judge, or you too will be judged.* A speck may blur your vision but a plank obstructs it, and judging others is a plank.

"Plank" Vision

Such planks become all you see. People with "plank" vision find that everywhere they look, they see only the flaws of others. Sawdust is the byproduct of construction with such wood planks. The sawdust of others becomes the focus. Those with "plank" vision recognize in others a byproduct of themselves.

Sawdust is not as obvious as specks or planks. People with planks walk about, totally unaware of their own blinders, all the while attempting to remove the various specks from the eyes of others. When you get a mental picture of it, you will see how silly and dangerous it is to think any of us can help anyone else while there are so many planks protruding from our own eyes. None of us would go to a blindfolded surgeon, now would we?

Our purpose is not to judge others with the truths we learn, but to judge ourselves. So often it is easier to listen to the sermon and apply it to someone next to us. Or to read a book for someone else. I have done it . . . I know. I'll read a book and think, *This is great! Boy, I know some people who really need to read this!*

My mind begins to race as I scheme how I'll get each person a copy of the book or how I'll find a way to read passages of it out loud to them.

Now that's all right if I just want to share something that has *already* helped me.

The only problem is I usually skip the "helped me" step and leap right into the process of helping or changing others. I become so busy reading the book for others that I fail to apply its truths to my own life. It is all right to help another when our eyes are clear. Jesus said first remove the plank from our own eye, then take care of the speck in our brother's eye. When the planks in our own eyes are removed, we will be able to see clearly again and our motives will be pure.

In addition to closet-cleaning we are going to add plank-removal to our list of conquests. Because it is difficult for us to go on even reading if we have planks in our eyes, I want you to pause now and think of anyone you feel a pressure to change, or of those you know that you have passed judgment upon. Let your mind travel as far as national leaders, circle back to pastors and leaders, then come as close as your own home. When you have searched your heart, let's join together in prayer.

Father, Your Word is a lamp unto our feet and a light unto our paths. It is so important that we be able to see that light. We repent of any tendency to judge others. Father, remove the measure of judgment against us as we sow mercy to others. Portion Your mercy to us as we now extend it to others.

Open our eyes and remove the planks that obstruct our vision. We know it is Your truth that makes us free. We realize that the discomfort we have experienced is because we felt it was our responsibility to change or judge our brothers and sisters. Father, You alone know the secrets of our hearts, and we release them into Your care. Amen.

(You may write their names here or in your journal as a record of their release.)

_____

_____

_____

(God doesn't mind us recording each other's names in our books . . . He records our names in His!)

What a relief! Now that we have laid down the heavy burden of measuring others, we can get on with the business of judging and measuring ourselves. God encourages us to judge ourselves to avoid *judgment ourselves*. It is our chance to grow and learn from our mistakes here and now. Hidden within each mistake is a seed of knowledge that, when planted in a repentant heart, produces the fruit necessary to prevent its recurrence. We judge ourselves by the truth and standard of God's Word.

When I first began to search my heart I was overwhelmed with guilt and discouragement at what I found there. My heart seemed to have become a brood of vipers overnight. The deeper I looked, the darker it appeared. Why wouldn't I become discouraged? I was excavating without any light.

A heart search must be conducted by the light of God's Word. His Word is a lamp unto our feet, showing us which paths to walk on. Under the guidance and counsel of God's Word, we can know the answer when we see the problem. His Word is a light that shines into the darkness and exposes it. I had been probing my heart according to the darkness of my own counsel, and consequently I found myself in a forest of despair. My motives were good, but my methods were wrong. In this book, we will search our hearts by His light and He will show us the paths we are to take.

How Do We Compare?

WE CAN ONLY rightly divide truth when we have first applied it to our own hearts. For too long we have not had accurate information by which to measure ourselves. We have assessed ourselves by those around us and by our own past failures and successes. God does not measure us this way. Paul warns us:

> We do not dare to classify or compare ourselves with some who commend themselves. When they measure themselves by themselves and compare themselves with themselves, they are not wise.
>
> —2 CORINTHIANS 10:12

Paul was pretty bold, and if he says he wouldn't dare to *do* something, then it is definitely something we also need to avoid. Yet, often we have a tendency to compare ourselves with others. Our reasoning goes something like this: *Well, I do more than Sally does! She only has one child and doesn't even sing in the choir!* or *I don't gossip like Susie, that girl is never off the phone!* These exchanges may

29

temporarily ease our consciences. Though it may be true, Sally and Susie are *not* God's standard for our lives. God says this line of reasoning and justification is not wise.

He wants us to have a head-on collision with truth, not with someone in the choir loft. I have learned that when I am confronted with truth, it is best not to defend myself but to submit to it. Hidden in the initial pain of impact is the power to rise from my captivity.

Deception comes in when we resist truth. In a confrontation with truth, reasoning and justifying ourselves will lead straight into deception. When the truth of God's Word is applied, we can see with our eyes, hear with our ears, and know with our hearts.

Since we are dealing with the topic, *the true measure of a woman,* truth will be our constant companion. It is time to strike the balance between truth and worth. Proverbs 11:1 tells us:

> The LORD abhors dishonest scales, but accurate weights are
> his delight.

God hates dishonest or unjust measurements. He delights in honest, just, and fair ones. Women have been measured by dishonest scales for far too long.

WEIGHTS AND MEASURES

A SCALE IS the unit that measures weight or a rate of exchange, matching value for value and worth for worth. For example, if a dollar buys a fourth of a pound of jelly beans, you would place a quarter-pound weight on one side of the scale and add jelly beans to the other side until both sides balanced.

An honest scale is a symbol of justice, representing equality, equity and fairness. When a scale is balanced it is considered to be just. When a scale of justice is unbalanced, it has been tipped unfairly in one direction by influence or deceptive weights. Its calculations are no longer trustworthy.

We have all heard the term, "worth its weight in gold." This saying has its origins in ancient times, when valuables were placed on just such a scale and weighed in proportion to an identical measure of purest gold.

In order to try this form of measure today, you would first determine the exact weight of the item in question, then place an accurate representation of this weight on one side of the scale and place gold on the other side until both balanced. Pound for pound, the value of the item being weighed could be proven equal to that of gold.

I believe Proverbs 11:1 has both a practical and a spiritual application. To better understand the spiritual application we must first gain a good understanding of its natural application. In the practical sense, this scripture refers to *dishonest scales,* which describe the fraudulent selling and buying by use of scales or balances. God is exposing a practice that has been conducted in secret, today and throughout the centuries.

Vendors would tinker with scales and misrepresent weights to take advantage of their customers. For example, if you were to request one pound of flour from a dishonest vendor, he would place the lightened version of a one-pound weight on one side of the scale and your flour on the other side.

As you watched, he would add or deduct flour until the scales appeared to balance. Your flour would be transferred into a sack or container and you'd be sent on your way. As you walked away, you would have no way of knowing that your sack was shy a few ounces of flour.

You would have been certain the measure of it was accurate. After all, you watched just to make sure—but the merchant's one-pound balance weight actually weighed just fourteen ounces. You paid for more flour than you received.

In this manner, merchants were able to increase their profit margin. When you went home and dumped what you thought was a pound of flour into your recipe for bread, you found out there was a problem. The only way to avoid this sort of theft was to go to a reputable source and make accurate weights of your own. But even using your own weights, the merchants would argue that their weights were right and yours were too heavy.

DECEITFUL GAIN

MERCHANTS ALSO used this practice when they purchased grain from farmers. For their suppliers they had another set of weights. These weights were heavier than what they actually represented. For example, a one-pound weight might really weigh eighteen ounces. Farmers would sell their grain to the merchants to market, usually in large quantities. A measure that was off just a little would mean great profit to the merchant—and great but unknown loss to the farmer.

If a farmer brought in one hundred pounds of grain, he had no way of knowing its weight because he had no scales. This put him in the position of having to trust the justice of the merchant's scale. If the merchant said his hundred pounds of wheat weighed only ninety-five pounds, the farmer accepted it.

The merchant had received a bonus five pounds. If ten farmers came to him with a hundred pounds of grain each, at the close of the day this dishonest merchant would have acquired fifty pounds of grain he never paid for. He would turn around and sell it for more than what it was worth.

In ancient times, the only way to avoid this sort of deception was to have your own method of weighing your goods before you brought them to market.

This theft was not limited to small units of measure and purchases but encompassed sales with all units of measurement. Though practiced in secret, God warned against it in Leviticus 19:35:

> Do not use dishonest standards when measuring length, weight or quantity.

This form of dishonesty had been used to move ancestral boundary lines, rob farmers, and cheat consumers. God wanted

His children to be protected from this treachery. His people had naively trusted the dishonest merchants for too long. After the Lord's warning, measures were taken to protect consumers and suppliers from such dishonest trade. Accurate and standardized weights were established.

It is no different today. If you do not have an accurate weight of measurement, you will probably receive far less than what you paid for. If you don't have any accurate appraisal of your worth, you will sell out for far less.

Dishonest weights will also cause you to sell yourself short. Like the farmer, you will have been cheated. Or like a consumer, you will go through life thinking you are purchasing a pound, when you have actually been shortchanged. If you accept the merchant's measure, or value, as accurate you will never know you've been undersold.

To counteract this deception, we will need to go to an honest source and get some accurate measuring weights, ones that have not been tampered with or hollowed out by the merchants of this world. Our culture has lied to us about the true measure of a woman, selling us far short of our worth.

AN ACCURATE MEANS OF MEASUREMENT

OUR SEARCH is for an accurate measure, one that balances truth *and* worth. It must be pure, incorruptible, solid, and tested. There is only one source to find this type of measure. It is found in the treasury of God's counsel and wisdom. Once we find this measure, we must use it to assure that we will never again be sold something less valuable.

This measure will consist of truth. For it is *God's truth* that sets us free. Let's pattern our quest for truth after Solomon's search. Although he was the wisest man ever to live, he was the first to admit he did not hold within himself the answers. Here is his statement of purpose:

I, the Teacher, was king over Israel in Jerusalem. I devoted myself to study and to explore by wisdom all that is done under heaven.

—ECCLESIASTES 1:12–13

Solomon set his mind on the pursuit of wisdom and to understand the meaning behind everything God had made. As a king who reigned during peaceful times, he was able to devote himself entirely to this endeavor. It is interesting to note that this was his quest even after God appeared to Solomon in a dream:

The Lord appeared to Solomon during the night in a dream, and God said, "Ask for whatever you want me to give you."

—1 KINGS 3:5

Can you imagine the intensity of this moment? What if Solomon's heart had not been prepared?

I've said and done some pretty wild stuff in my dreams. He might have asked for a "good thing," yet missed the "God thing." He could have asked that Jerusalem would prosper and that his kingdom would expand. He could have asked for the health of his children and wives. But he did not.

Solomon's request was a reflection of what God desired in the king of Israel.

Solomon answered:

Give your servant a discerning heart to govern your people and to distinguish between right and wrong. For who is able to govern this great people of yours?

—1 KINGS 3:9

This was not the answer of a know-it-all. Solomon was humbled by the gargantuan task set before him. The Lord was pleased with Solomon's response. So God blessed him with even more:

Since you have asked for this and not for long life or wealth for yourself, nor have asked for the death of your enemies but for discernment in administering justice, I will do what you have asked. I will give you a wise and discerning heart, so that there will never have been anyone like you, nor will there ever be. Moreover, I will give you what you have not asked for—both riches and honor—so that in your lifetime you will have no equal among kings.

—1 KINGS 3:11–13

THE NECESSITY OF WISDOM

NOT ONLY would Solomon be the wisest man who had ever lived, but he would rise above his peers and his wisdom would outlive him to surpass the wisdom of all future generations of kings and leaders. With all our technology, computers, and databases, Solomon was still wiser. He had none of these high-tech resources to draw from. He drew from the counsel of the Creator.

At first this claim might seem incredulous, but we can be certain it is indeed the truth because it was made by God. If we are awed by how this could possibly be true, it is because we are using a flawed measurement of wisdom.

There is a mistaken impression that the accumulation of knowledge is wisdom. If this were indeed true, to what lofty pinnacle has this vast knowledge brought us? We live in a culture brimming with excess, poverty, perversion, violence, and wickedness. Ours is a generation of people who are self-ruled and haughty. Our world is riddled with disease, plague, want, and war. It is obvious that in our pursuit of knowledge, we have forsaken truth.

Without wisdom we may possess all the knowledge this world may offer and still remain fools. It is not more technology or knowledge that we need. Our souls cry out for wisdom. Wisdom is the ability to apply knowledge, experience, and truth, while retaining proper relationship with God and man.

Wisdom gives us eyes to see and ears to hear. Only then will we recognize truth when we find it. In the pursuit of knowledge we have strayed from the path of wisdom and discretion. We have allowed knowledge to exalt us to the realm of self-rule. We have become a generation of self-ruled, self-motivated *fools*. "The fool says in his heart, 'There is no God'" (Ps. 14:1). We may acknowledge God's existence, while we live as though He did not.

Solomon sensed his overwhelming need for wisdom. As ruler of God's people, he bore more than a national government upon his shoulders. He set his heart to make wisdom his lifelong pursuit. He held a royal position in which his riches were unfathomable, his influence worldwide, his authority and power respected and feared. Kings from all over the world brought tribute to Solomon in deference to his wisdom and excellence.

Solomon lived free from the fear of sudden death. God had promised him a long life, as long as he walked in His ways. It was in this boundless and prosperous atmosphere that Solomon expanded himself to experience, observe, and encompass many facets of life.

In all his endeavors he possessed God's wisdom to accurately judge the merit of whatever lay before him, both in this life and eternally. He systematically tried by trial and error the worth of the natural resources and wealth he found under the sun.

Though we don't have the time and resources of Solomon, his wisdom is recorded so that we might continually benefit from it. In the next chapter we will study the pattern of his search and contrast it with our natural lives. Likewise, we will apply truth to various social, religious, and cultural concepts of womanhood.

Before going on, please answer these questions:

How old are you? _____

How do you measure or see yourself? _____

_____

_____

*How did you measure yourself ten years ago?*_____

_____

_____

*How did you measure yourself twenty-five years ago?*_____

_____

_____

(This question applies to all over thirty.)

*What qualities do you value in your friends?*_____

_____

_____

_____

_____

*What do you consider the most valuable quality about you?*____

_____

*What is your most **unique** characteristic?*_____

_____

_____

(The last two answers may be the same.)

*What is the most valuable and precious thing you possess?*_____

_____

_____

*How would society classify or measure you?*_____

_____

_____

_____

God is

more concerned with

our condition than our

comfort.

4

Solomon's Search

*I know that whatever God does, it shall be forever. Nothing can
be added to it, and nothing taken from it. God does it, that men
should fear before Him.*

—*ECCLESIASTES 3:14, NKJV*

WE WILL trace the path of Solomon's search. As a
young child he was tutored in the ways and wisdom
of the Lord by his mother, Bathsheba. He was her
closest and most treasured son. David had promised her that
Solomon would sit upon the throne and succeed him (1 Kings
1:30). The Lord had loved Solomon from the moment of his
birth and sent confirmation of Solomon's destiny by the mouth
of the prophet, Nathan (2 Sam. 12:24–25).

In the light of this, Bathsheba raised Solomon from infancy
to be set apart as a prince and ruler over God's people. She
instructed him daily in the statues and fear of the Lord.

Solomon confirms this repeatedly in Proverbs:

> When I was a boy in my father's house, still tender, and an only child of my mother, he taught me and said, "Lay hold of my words with all your heart; keep my commands and you will live . . . My son, keep your father's commands and do not forsake your mother's teaching."
> —PROVERBS 4:3–4, 6:20

Solomon's father gave him commandments and his mother taught him. David would speak God's laws or principles, then Bathsheba would explain to the young Solomon how they were to be applied to life. Her words bore insight into relationships, gave warning and instruction, and imparted an even deeper desire within Solomon for wisdom.

When Solomon became king he was still a young man. In his exploration of all that was under sun, he began with the pursuit of pleasure. In his own words:

> I thought in my heart, "Come now, I will test you with pleasure to find out what is good." . . . I tried cheering myself with wine, and embracing folly—my mind still guiding me with wisdom. I wanted to see what was worthwhile for men to do under heaven during the few days of their lives.
> —ECCLESIASTES 2:1, 3

HAVE WE MISSED ANYTHING?

DOESN'T THAT sound like a lot of us? We were raised by parents who instructed us the best they knew how, teaching us right from wrong in the hope that we would learn from their mistakes. But most of us, as soon as we were on our own, pursued pleasure. We just had to find out what we were missing.

After all, we were eighteen and free to vote and make our own decisions! It was now legal for many of us to drink and we wanted to cheer ourselves with wine and embrace folly. Sin *does* have pleasure for a season . . . a short one. It wasn't long before we decided we wanted more out of life. We wanted to make a difference, raise a family, achieve professional and personal goals. So as Solomon did, we moved on to the pursuit of achievement.

> I undertook great projects: I built houses for myself and planted vineyards. I made gardens and parks and planted all kinds of fruit trees in them. I made reservoirs to water groves of flourishing trees. I bought male and female slaves and had other slaves who were born in my house. I also owned more herds and flocks than anyone in Jerusalem before me. I amassed silver and gold for myself, and the treasure of kings and provinces. I acquired men and women singers, and a harem as well—the delights of the heart of man. I became greater by far than anyone in Jerusalem before me. In all this my wisdom stayed with me.
> —ECCLESIASTES 2:4–9

Initially Solomon was overjoyed by his success. He enjoyed completing projects and living in his many houses. He feasted on the fruit he had cultivated and shared beautiful parks with his subjects. There was an ever-increasing army of male and female slaves who lived to fulfill his every desire. His herds of livestock outnumbered everyone else's. He gathered for himself a treasury of gold, silver, riches, and lands. He surrounded himself with the best of the world's culture in the form of art and music. He enjoyed the unlimited sensual pleasure of a harem. He was greater than anyone before him. In all this, wisdom remained his constant companion.

> I denied myself nothing my eyes desired; I refused my heart no pleasure. My heart took delight in all my work, and this was the reward for all my labor.
> —ECCLESIASTES 2:10

He denied himself nothing! His heart delighted in his work.

This delight was in itself a reward for his labor. He loved being king, he loved his work, and he loved all that surrounded him! It brought him fulfillment . . . for a season. Soon *having* the most, *doing* the most, and *being* the most were not enough for Solomon.

> Yet when I surveyed all that my hands had done and what I had toiled to achieve, everything was meaningless, a chasing after the wind; nothing was gained under the sun.
> —ECCLESIASTES 2:11

LIKE CHASING THE WIND

WHAT DID HE MEAN, *nothing was gained?* Solomon was *the best.* With wisdom's guidance Solomon looked closer and decided all his achievements were as meaningless as chasing the wind. Think about it! The greatest and wisest king's achievements were comparable to chasing after something one could never capture.

The winds of time had blown by Solomon and reminded him that he was but a mortal and would someday die. In contrast, the wind would continue to encircle the earth, blowing and dispersing the dust of man's achievements from one generation to the next.

This revelation caused Solomon to despise what he had once loved.

> I hated all the things I had toiled for under the sun, because I must leave them to the one who comes after me. And who knows whether he will be a wise man or a fool? Yet he will have control over all the work into which I have poured my effort and skill under the sun. This too is meaningless. So my heart began to despair over all my toilsome labor under the sun. For a man may do his work with wisdom, knowledge and skill, and then he must leave all he owns to someone who has not worked for it. This too is meaningless and a great misfortune.
> —ECCLESIASTES 2:18–21

The wealth, riches, and lands he had toiled in joy to accumulate had now become a source of vexation to this great king. What he had worked for would eventually be lost. All he had tenderly and diligently cultivated could be squandered in the hands of a foolish king. He realized he could not hold on, he must pass it on. All he had accomplished by years of labor would endure but a moment after he was gone. In contrast, Solomon noted:

> I know that whatever God does, it shall be forever. Nothing can be added to it, and nothing taken from it. God does it, that men should fear before Him.
> —ECCLESIASTES 3:14, NKJV

Although Solomon was the greatest king who had ever lived or ever would live, what he had built would not endure. He saw that it would all be swept away. He realized that even as the greatest and wisest king, he could only hold it but a moment. No man could ever hold onto it. Yet the stars and heavens shining above the works of Solomon remained steadfast. The sun, moon, and stars that lit his kingdom would continue to shine long after Solomon's descendants rested in their graves.

Why would God allow this great frustration in a king He loved? Why did He let Solomon enjoy all he had acquired, only to expose the futility of it? Solomon gave the answer: *God does it, that men should fear before Him.*

It was humbling for Solomon to find out that all his wisdom could not preserve his possessions or lengthen his days. All his glory was like the grass—one day splendid, green, and life-giving and the next cut down and swept away. The Book of Ecclesiastes is his lament of this earthly, temporary life. He had glimpsed God's everlasting glory and wisdom and found his own glory waning.

At the end of his life, Solomon concluded:

> "Meaningless! Meaningless!" says the Teacher. "Everything is meaningless!"
> —ECCLESIASTES 12:8

How many times have you ended up disillusioned and disappointed by something that once brought you happiness? Like Solomon, each of us at one time or another has thought, *If only I achieved this or had that, I would be happy!* Only we discover that once we achieve these things, we still are not satisfied. Then we become discouraged because we thought these things would bring us happiness, not disappointment. We have lost the boost of momentum which comes when one pursues a dream.

Ask yourself the following questions and record your answers:

Over the course of your life, what did you pursue, thinking it would bring fulfillment, but instead left you disappointed? _____

_____

_____

_____

What goals are you pursuing now? _____

_____

_____

_____

Will you be happy once you achieve them? _____

It is important to note that there is nothing wrong with having goals and dreams. God made us with the creative capacity to dream. It is equally important to note that outside of the provision of God, none of us is able to enjoy the blessings He gives us.

Moreover, when God gives any man wealth and possessions, and enables him to enjoy them, to accept his lot and be happy in his work—this is a gift of God.

—ECCLESIASTES 5:19

THE RIGHT PERSPECTIVE ON "THINGS"

GOD GIVES wealth, possessions, and contentment. Outside of His provision we may have "things" but not peace. This means we cannot enjoy them. Often those with the greatest possessions are tormented with the most worry. They cannot rest and enjoy what they have because they are consumed with thinking of ways that they might safeguard and even expand their riches. Then there is another torment that plagues them. Though they have much, they notice there are those who have even more. They strive, trying to gain as much as their neighbor, and so are never satisfied with what they have in their hands. They lose what they possess, either by holding it too tightly or by grasping for more.

This is a telltale sign of those who have measured themselves by what they have. Possessions are a deceptive measure of worth. There is no lasting stability because a person's worth is not dependent on the increase or decrease of possessions.

This mentality breeds only fear and insecurity. It would mean a person's worth and value would be assigned to something that is inevitably out of his or her control. There are also theft and calamity to consider, not to mention the warnings contained in Proverbs:

> Cast but a glance at riches, and they are gone, for they will surely sprout wings and fly off to the sky like an eagle.
> —PROVERBS 23:5

This illustrates just how fleeting and elusive riches can be—sprouting wings and flying off like an eagle. Eagles are hard to catch once they have taken flight.

Proverbs 11:28 tells us, "Whoever trusts in his riches will fall, but the righteous will thrive like a green leaf." Riches cannot be trusted; they are here today and gone tomorrow. Riches in and of themselves are not wrong; it is the trusting in them that is wrong.

The righteous trust in God, not in riches, and therefore thrive. Thriving means more than just existing. To thrive means to prosper, flourish, succeed, advance, increase, bloom, and blossom!

All man could ever want is found in God's righteousness. This is not just a temporary state, because Proverbs 8:18 promises, "With me are riches and honor, enduring wealth and prosperity." With God the blessings endure because they are His. With Him we have a temporary and eternal reward of joy and contentment. It is independent of what we have or do not have, own or do not own.

> Then he said to them, "Watch out! Be on your guard against all kinds of greed; a man's life does not consist in the abundance of his possessions."
>
> —LUKE 12:15

It is an urgent warning that not only do we have to look out for but also guard against measuring ourselves by what we have. It is so subtle that it can creep in without our awareness. It is preached by almost every television commercial. Its lie is propagated by sitcoms, movies, and magazines. The world promises that riches will give you everything you want, make you beautiful, fill your house with the best of everything, surround you with friends, give you influence and power, and secure the future for you and your loved ones. But it is a lie.

Our lives are of a much greater worth than *things* and, therefore, our lives cannot be measured by things. If our worth were equal to a whole world of things, then God would not have ransomed us with the life of His only Son. Instead, He would have ransomed us with the boundless riches of heaven, where the riches are so immense that gold paves the streets. In God's eyes, our worth is far more precious than gold.

BALANCING THE BLESSINGS

JEALOUSLY COVETING the possessions of others is still measuring ourselves by *what we think we should have*. When I was first married John and I lived in Dallas. We attended a church where financial prosperity was equated with righteousness. Everyone was busy pursuing the blessings of God!

At first I was repulsed by this. I had been raised in a well-off family and had long ago realized that money did not necessarily make a person happy.

All the women in my circle of friends were draped in furs and expensive jewelry. It seemed that every Sunday a new fur coat would appear. As we left the service one afternoon my husband complimented a friend of ours: "That's a beautiful fur coat you gave your wife!"

"God wants nothing but the best for my wife!" the smiling gentleman responded.

John and I were silent for awhile in the cold car. Then John turned to me and said, "Honey, I need to buy you a fur jacket!"

Was I hearing him right? We didn't even have a house!

"I don't *need* one," I protested weakly.

I certainly did not need a fur jacket . . . but I was beginning to *want* one. So what if we didn't have a house yet? We were young. I would look so elegant in my new fur jacket as I walked into church, shopped at the mall, and wandered the grocery aisles. No one would look down on me when I wore my fur jacket! All the store clerks would be attentive!

I smiled at my sweet husband and kept all these thoughts to myself. Inwardly I reasoned, *If that man's wife deserves the best, surely I deserve the best! My grandmother has minks and my mother has a magnificent full-length lynx coat. What's a simple fox jacket?*

The following Sunday morning a couple two years younger than John and I—who were then twenty-three and twenty-four—showed up at church with a wife in fur.

I snapped. Now I didn't *think* I wanted a fur; I now felt I *needed* one. I began to scan the Dallas papers for fur sales and estate auctions. I began to drop hints to my husband that I had changed my mind about a fur. Christmas was coming and I needed to be in fur!

Then one night John and I slipped into a furrier shop just

before closing time. There it was—a crystal fox jacket. I tried it on. It was stunning. Then I looked at the price tag—$1,600! I quickly peeled the jacket off and hung it back up on the rack.

"What's the matter?" John questioned. "Don't you like it?"

"Yes, I like it, but *look at the price!*" I whispered back.

"Try it on again," John encouraged.

"No, I don't want to." I felt uncomfortable and conspicuous.

At this point a salesperson came over and asked if we needed assistance. The clerk looked a little doubtful, as if John and I were a bit too young and underdressed to be serious shoppers.

In an irritated and snobby tone, the salesperson asked, "Have you found something you like?"

"Yes," John replied. "I want to buy my wife that fur."

I was shocked and feeling a little sick to my stomach.

"No!" I protested, now in earnest.

"Yes," John insisted as he took the fur from me and handed it to the salesperson.

"How will you pay for it?" I asked.

"I'll put it on a store charge," John confidently explained. He was determined.

I wasn't excited or happy at all. If anything, I was a little scared. We had committed never to go in debt. If we didn't have the money, we believed we weren't supposed to buy it. John had gone over to a desk to apply for the store charge. We were compromising something we both had agreed on in order to get me something I didn't even need—and now didn't even want!

I prayed, "God, please forgive me and somehow stop this from happening! I have made my husband feel as though he doesn't really love and appreciate me unless he clothes me in fur. It is manipulation. Forgive me!"

I wandered closer to the desk where John and the salesperson were going over his application for credit, and John looked upset.

"We can't authorize this purchase; you don't have any credit," the salesperson stated.

"Let me get on the phone with them," my husband asserted.

Now not only was his love for me in question but also his ability to provide for me. After failing to convince the credit people that his income justified a purchase of this amount, John hung up.

I had started to cry and had stepped out into the mall. John saw me and thought I was crying because I couldn't have the fur.

"Now look—*my wife is crying!* I can't believe you won't authorize this!" John exclaimed in disgust as he stormed out of the store.

Never had I seen my husband act like this. It was not his nature to behave in this manner. As we hurried out of the closing mall, he assured me, "Honey, *we are going to get you a fur!*" It had become a badge of conquest.

"No," I softly answered. "I don't *want* one anymore."

In the car we talked about the pressures we had both felt to appear to be something we were not. I apologized for my part in the whole thing and assured John that I knew he loved me. I made John promise *not to buy me a fur!*

WHAT I LEARNED FROM THE FUR EPISODE

IT IS NOT that furs are bad, or that I am an animal activist. The prospect of owning a fur had held the wrong place in my heart. I wanted to project an image of wealth. The prospect of owning a fur had exposed an unjust balance of materialism in my life.

Not only had I been measuring myself by what I had, but when I saw other Christians blessed I sought to get what they had for myself.

> And I saw that all labor and all achievement spring from man's envy of his neighbor. This too is meaningless, a chasing after the wind.
>
> —ECCLESIASTES 4:4

Why are these pursuits comparable to chasing the wind? Because even if I do get whatever I desire, I will soon see something else that I want. I'll be forever reaching, never fulfilled.

After we moved from Dallas, John and I returned to minister at a different church. We were staying in the home of some dear friends and had stopped by a very exclusive department store to get them a "thank you" gift. When we walked in, there was an elaborate display of men's ties that caught John's eye. There were two ties that he was particularly fond of, and he couldn't decide between the two. After a few minutes of deliberation, John had an idea. He would buy one tie and I would get him the other for Christmas.

At first I wasn't too keen on this; I liked picking out presents for people so I could share in their surprise. I told him I'd think about it. However, I could see that he really wanted that tie. John purchased the one tie while I ran upstairs to see a friend of ours who worked in another department of the store. I returned to the tie counter and bought the other tie. As the salesman carefully wrapped it for me, I started feeling grieved. I thought, *What's going on? This is my spending money, and I'm buying a present for my husband. Do I have to pray about every purchase?* I took the bag from the salesman and started up the escalator. Halfway up, I felt deeply grieved. I saw John waiting at the top of the escalator.

"What's wrong?" he asked.

"John, I bought you the tie, but I am grieved over it."

"I am grieved as well. I think you should return it."

We went down together and returned the tie. I'm sure the poor salesman thought we were nuts. As I placed the money back in my purse, I heard the Holy Spirit say to me, "The blessings I give you will come with no sorrow. The ones you take for yourself will cause you sorrow."

I made note of the lesson, still wondering why buying a tie for my husband was such a big deal.

A few weeks later we both found out why. John was in Chicago preaching. After the service a man asked John to come by his men's clothing store. The following day, the pastor took John by the store and the man blessed John with twelve ties, several shirts, and a gorgeous winter coat! I believe that if we had purchased the tie for ourselves in Dallas, God would not have moved upon this man's heart to give to John in such a generous way. We would have grabbed our *one* tie when God wanted to give us *twelve* ties.

OBEDIENCE, NOT FORMULA

THIS DOES NOT mean that every time God has told me not to get something I received the same item in large quantities at a later date. It is not a formula but obedience that God blesses. He is more concerned with our *condition* than our *comfort*. He knows He can bless obedience, because the obedient know that fulfillment is not found in the blessings but in obedience to the One who blesses. This is why Paul said:

> But godliness with contentment is great gain.
> —1 TIMOTHY 6:6

True and great riches are found in godliness with contentment. Too often I have picked up a magazine or catalog featuring the latest trends in home decorating, overwhelmed by the urge, *I must redecorate in this color scheme!* Then reason would grab me as I realized I was perfectly content with what I had . . . *until I saw something else.* I decided to fast—stop reading these magazines for awhile. In place of decorating magazines I put out my Bible.

Whenever I read my Bible I felt stronger and refreshed, not discontent. It was amazing how much of my thought life had been dominated by the attractive contents of these magazines. When I did pick them up again, the magazines had no hold on me. They were in the right perspective. I could enjoy their ideas without a sense of frustration.

Like me, you may be surrounded by forces that arouse a desire for more in your life. It may be the lifestyle of the rich and famous. (Why is it that we never see the heartbreak behind the facade?) Or it may simply be a friend who has everything you want. Only you know your heart and the passions that may drive it.

One truth is certain—*you are not what you own.* A woman cannot be measured by what she possesses. Not by her home, car, jewelry, or things.

Pray with me:

Father God, Forgive me for the times I have measured my self-worth by what I possess. Forgive me for trying to hold on to things. Forgive me for the times I grabbed and reached for more. Search my heart and expose any jealousy by the light of Your Word. Quicken in me the discernment to realize when greed is trying to attack me with discontentment. God, I want only the blessings You provide for me. Develop godliness with contentment in my life. Forgive me for making those around me feel that the measure of their affections was in the gifts they gave. I cast off the false weight of possessions and press on to Your true measure. I refuse to trust in riches. I place my trust in You. Let me thrive with the righteous! In Jesus' name, Amen.

God weighs our hearts

by what He places in our hands.

He measures us by what we have . . . not

by what we lack.

5

"It's Not Fair!"

It will be like a man going on a journey, who called his servants and entrusted his property to them. To one he gave five talents of money, to another two talents, and to another one talent, each according to his ability. Then he went on his journey.
—MATTHEW 25:14-15

IF ALL OF US are created equal . . . then it isn't fair!" This wail of protest would usually float into my kitchen. Sometimes it was toy disputes. "I had it first!" or "He got more!" Other times it was a game or sports conflict, "He cheated!" or "It's my turn!"

Whenever possible I would act as though I had not heard. I wanted to remain uninvolved. I would pause to determine just how far it would escalate. Would it be a minor scuffle involving only words? Or an opportunity for bloodshed? I listened silently to the discourse; if it seemed they could resolve it on their own, I wouldn't comment. There were other times, though, when words gave way to tears, bites, and fists. I'd quit what I was doing and run upstairs to mediate or terminate the play time.

With four boys there have been many such occasions, often in a single day. I try to stay out of their disagreements, first because I always hope they will resolve them and second, I dreaded walking upstairs or outside to solve it. Usually I would resort to yelling a question like, "Are you guys playing sweet?" or, "Is everybody sharing?" I know they are obvious and silly questions that just encourage responses like, "I am—but he's not!"

When my oldest son, Addison, began school his perception of fairness expanded to a whole new dimension. He became the self-appointed administrator of justice. This job description included seating arrangements, "You sat next to Dad last night; tonight is Alexander's turn," or, "I'm oldest so I should sit in the front seat of the car." It spread to the domain of food, where fairness was scrutinized according to his preferences. If it was a portion of ice cream, it was not fair to give them all the same amount; after all, he was the oldest! If it was beans, it wasn't fair to give him more, because he didn't like them.

The fairness checks and balances bred clashes whenever there was a perceived violation. This all began to wear thin on me. It seemed everything I asked wasn't fair and everyone he knew wasn't fair! One night in response to my request for him to help pick up the TV room, he protested, "It's not fair! I didn't play with all these toys, and I always end up putting away more!"

I took a deep breath and sat him down. I let him know I fully understood how he felt. I shared how I often felt it wasn't fair that I had to clean up messes I didn't make and wash clothes I hadn't soiled.

He smiled and patted me, "Let's make the babies pick all the toys up and we'll go read a book!"

I could see I wasn't getting anywhere. He needed a new perspective. I asked him this question: "Was it fair that Jesus died on the cross when He had done nothing wrong?"

He looked perplexed and his tone changed, "No."

"God didn't ask Jesus to die because it was *fair;* He did it because it would be *just*. Jesus died to fulfill the punishment for man's sin. Addison, life is not fair, but God is just."

It was one of those quiet and precious moments when you see in your child's eyes a truth implanted. When you know beyond a shadow of a doubt that your child has understood what you've said.

He quietly nodded his blond head, hugged me, and began picking up the toys, calling to his brothers, "Here, you guys, big brother will show you how!"

LIFE'S NOT FAIR!

HOW OFTEN do we question the fairness of things? I am certain it's too often to count. God is eternally just, but at times I've questioned His immediate perspective on fairness. Because He is God, all-knowing, omnipotent, omnipresent, I mentally know that from an eternal perspective His wisdom, justice, and sense of right and truth are above question. I read my Bible and I'm awed by the perfection of His wisdom.

It was not the "Big Picture" that I questioned. My questions arose over what I perceived as apparent injustices—the ones that weren't mentioned in the Bible, ones I deemed as unfair from my vantage and network of limited knowledge, experience, and life span. It seemed at birth some began with more than others, as if they had a head start before I had even begun.

Life wasn't fair like Monopoly, where everyone at least starts out at the same time and with the same amount of money. Mishap could be expected under the care of game dice, but not when God was in charge and making the rules. I thought He should be fairer.

I was frustrated as I tried to judge between fair and unfair. I quickly surmised that I needed to change my perspective on fairness. I was judging things from Milton Bradley's perspective and I needed to change over to God's. Jesus gave a parable to describe the kingdom perspective:

It will be like a man going on a journey, who called his

57

servants and entrusted his property to them. To one he gave five talents of money, to another two talents, and to another one talent, each according to his ability. Then he went on his journey.

—MATTHEW 25:14–15

This distribution of talents was not equal (as in Monopoly) or what most would consider fair (as in equal opportunity). They were portioned out according to individual ability. They were the master's property to do with as he felt best. He was leaving and needed to know that his property would be treated as though he were still there. He gave it proportionally to those who would use it wisely.

When you entrust someone with something of value, it is totally at their disposal, so it is important that you know their heart. Let's look at the response of these servants:

The man who had received the five talents went at once and put his money to work and gained five more. So also, the one with the two talents gained two more. But the man who had received the one talent went off, dug a hole in the ground and hid his master's money.

—MATTHEW 25:16–18

The first man went immediately and put to work the talents entrusted to him. The man entrusted with two talents put his to work also, and gained two more.

But the man given only one talent "went off, dug a hole . . . and hid his master's money." This exhibits a major attitude problem. He did not even try to increase what had been entrusted to him. He saw what the others had received, stormed off, offended, and buried the one he had. His actions expressed the contempt in his heart: "You won't get anything from me! I'm not going to spend myself to benefit you. You gave me one talent and one is all you'll get back! You ask too much of me! How dare you only give me one!"

After a long time the master of those servants returned and settled accounts with them.

—MATTHEW 25:19

Notice it was a long time before the master came back. Often only the course of time will reveal the true nature or character of a person. There had been plenty of time for him to change his attitude. If this had been just a minor offense, there would have been ample time for him to repent, resolve the offense, and unearth the talent. Then he could have invested it in some manner, but he did not. His attitude revealed a deep-seated heart condition.

A HARVEST OF THE HEART

GOD KNEW his heart when he gave him the one talent. God patiently waits for the harvest of the heart. Look at the harvest evidenced by the response of the first and second men. You can hear their excitement and joy at the master's return:

> The man who had received the five talents brought the other five. "Master," he said, "you entrusted me with five talents. See, I have gained five more."
>
> His master replied, "Well done, good and faithful servant! You have been faithful with a few things; I will put you in charge of many things. Come and share your master's happiness!"
>
> The man with the two talents also came. "Master," he said, "you entrusted me with two talents; see, I have gained two more."
>
> His master replied, "Well done, good and faithful servant! You have been faithful with a few things; I will put you in charge of many things. Come and share your master's happiness!"
>
> —MATTHEW 25:20–23

These two servants were pronounced "good and faithful." You

59

can hear their master's pleasure with them. He blesses them with greater authority over even more! He knows they have perceived his heart and trusted him; therefore, he can trust them. *Those who trust can be trusted.* This excitement and joy are in a stark contrast to the last servant's reception:

> Then the man who had received the one talent came. "Master," he said, "I knew that you are a hard man, harvesting where you have not sown and gathering where you have not scattered seed. So I was afraid and went out and hid your talent in the ground. See, here is what belongs to you."
> —MATTHEW 25:24–25

What an attitude! Notice he comes last. He is not excited about his master's return. You can almost see him producing a dirty coin and casually throwing it at his master's feet or slapping it irreverently into his hand. The coins of the other servants were shiny and bright and presented in a manner that honored their master.

To this servant, returning the single talent, was a relief. He was glad to rid himself of his master's talent. He did not like caring for things that were not his own. To him, it had not been a talent filled with potential, but a burden. He did not trust his master and judged him harshly.

People who do not love . . . will fear. This man is afraid of his master because he doesn't know him. He comes to him last because he has the twisted perception of an offended, bitter man. He calls his master a hard man and accuses him of theft with his comment, *"harvesting where you have not sown and gathering where you have not scattered seed."* He was afraid his master might take from him, so he was careful to give nothing of himself. He was self-serving and, therefore, unwilling to do more than the minimum required. Look at his master's wise response:

> "You wicked, lazy servant! So you knew that I harvest where I have not sown and gather where I have not scattered seed? Well then, you should have put my money on deposit with

60

the bankers, so that when I returned I would have received it back with interest."

—MATTHEW 25:26–27

The master had weighed this servant's heart with this talent and found it to be wicked. He had entrusted him with good, but in the hands of this bitter, fearful, wicked servant, the good talent lay underground, hidden and dormant.

It is not how many talents you possess; it is what you do with those talents.

The Bible says God will test us with good, not evil. Jesus said it was a kingdom parable, so this master represents God the Father—not a wicked master, but a good one. You can trust and believe a good master.

This servant's perceptions were so warped that they caused him to doubt and fear. By the same harsh measure that he had judged his master, this wicked servant was now judged.

The master said to him, "If you really thought I was that way, then you should have behaved differently!"

This wicked servant suffered from "plank" sight and was not able to see his master for who he was. He was stripped of his talent and inherited the reward of an unbeliever:

> "Take the talent from him and give it to the one who has the ten talents. For everyone who has will be given more, and he will have an abundance. Whoever does not have, even what he has will be taken from him. And throw that worthless servant outside, into the darkness, where there will be weeping and gnashing of teeth."
>
> —MATTHEW 25:28–30

This man, once the servant of a great master, is cast outside of the blessings, privileges, and provisions of his master and into the company of the fearful and tormented.

That servant who knows his master's will and does not get

ready or does not do what his master wants will be beaten with many blows.

—LUKE 12:47

This servant knew his master's will. He had watched his master for years and knew what was being asked of him. Instead of fulfilling his master's will, or at least preparing himself for his return, he fulfills his own will and lives his own life. He dreads the day when he will be forced to settle accounts with his master. Afraid of what he will some day face, he does nothing.

INVESTING OUR TALENTS

GOD WEIGHS our hearts by what He places in our hands. He measures us by what we have . . . not by what we lack. He did not ask the second servant why his two talents had not made five. He knew proportionally that the first two men had both doubled the talents.

We are not measured by our limitations but by what we have the potential to do. The true measure of a woman does not lie in the number of her God-given talents and abilities, but in her faithfulness to use them to honor her Master.

> From everyone who has been given much, much will be demanded; and from the one who has been entrusted with much, much more will be asked.
>
> —LUKE 12:48

Notice the terminology, "entrusted with much." Again, Jesus is using a kingdom parable to teach His disciples. It is another story of servants left in charge in their master's absence. The demand, or accountability, is based on what was entrusted. If it was much, then much would be expected. If it was a little, then a little would be expected. Judgment is severe for those who know God's will, yet don't do it—more than for those who disobey out of ignorance. This makes the outcome *just*, even though the distribution of talents is not *equal*.

Remember, in God's kingdom *equal* is not always *just*, and *just* is not always *equal*. But individually the scales balance. God creates all us with equal opportunity but not with equal abilities. This is not based on age, gender, or race, but as God wills the distribution.

This truth is not only applicable to the natural and tangible. It extends to encompass a realm where worth exceeds the power of money, land, or ability. All of us vary in our talents and abilities. God does not judge variance; nor does He compare us one to another. He deals with us as individuals, and to each He gives at least one talent.

Don't limit this word *talent* to today's terminology, which defines it as "ability or skill." In this kingdom parable, it represents a unit of measure. It was used to measure gold (2 Sam. 12:30), silver (1 Kings 20:39), other metals, and commodities.

THE SAME TALENT OF FAITH

GOD ENTRUSTS each of us with a measure, or talent, of faith (Rom. 12:3). He gives each of us this measure because without faith, it is impossible to please God. When we become His children, each of us is granted an initial measure.

> But without faith it is impossible to please Him, for he who comes to God must believe that He is, and that He is a rewarder of those who diligently seek Him.
> —HEBREWS 11:6, NKJV

Why is it impossible to please God without faith? We find the answer in the same verse. We must come in faith, believing first that God exists, and second, that He is a rewarder of those who earnestly seek Him. Most believers do not doubt God's existence. Even Creation surrounds us with this declaration.

What they doubt is the second part; they doubt God's involvement with them on a personal level. They fear He won't reward them. They doubt His goodness. When we think like this, it causes us to hold back portions of our hearts and retain control of our lives. We do this because we are afraid. Fear torments us with questions: "What if I earnestly and diligently seek Him and He doesn't reward me?" "What if God rejects my efforts as not good enough?" "What if He asks for more than I can give Him?"

How does this attitude differ from that of the unfaithful servant? Wasn't he afraid that he wouldn't be rewarded? These fears represent the very seeds of his heart attitude. We will doubt God's goodness in areas where we are not sure of His character. This doubt will cause us to bury our talents in the soil of unbelief. Nothing reproduces or multiplies there; all remains lifeless and dormant.

Since a talent is a unit of measure, we can draw a parallel between this measure of faith and the allotment of talents. The talent of faith comes from God. It is incorruptible, since a talent represents a measure of gold or silver. First Peter 1:7 describes our faith as "of greater worth than gold, which perishes even though refined by fire." Faith does not perish in the fire; there, it is strengthened and purified.

Our faith is meant to be used. Its purpose is not to accumulate things but to receive and grow in the knowledge of God. It is given to each of us that we might mentally grasp and learn to handle the goodness of God. It is given so that we may experience Him as a rewarder of those who diligently seek Him.

Isn't that why you have this book in your hands? You want to know truth. He is the way, the truth, and the life. So what you really want to know more about is Him.

Notice the term, "diligently seek Him." He longs for us to simply seek Him, not what He can do for us. John and I have acquaintances whom we will not hear from for years. Then out of the blue, they will call! We will be so excited that they were thinking of us. We will talk awhile on the phone and then the real reason for their call comes out. They just joined an incredible direct-marketing company and they want a percentage of our phone bill! Or they just know God has laid a book on their hearts and they want us to help them get it published. Some, we help; others, we are not in a position to help. They say, "Let's get together for lunch!" As we hang up, we know we won't hear from them again because they got what they wanted.

Whenever this happens, a sadness hits our hearts. We thought these friends called because they wanted a relationship with us. We offered them our friendship, but they only wanted what we could do for them. I can't imagine that God doesn't experience this same sadness when we only contact Him when we need something from Him and turn down His offer of a deeper and more fulfilling relationship.

Then we have other friends, ones we have a relationship with. They may call and ask the same favors. But with them, it is different. There is no sadness. If we can, we are happy to help them. Regardless of whether or not we help them they are still our friends. We remain in fellowship because our relationship is not based on what we can do for them or what they can do for us.

GOD'S HEART

GOD WANTS to have this kind of relationship with us. He wants us to seek to know and grasp His heart. When we see His heart, we will find in its rich treasury whatever we have need of.

To do this, we must unearth our talent of faith from its dormancy of fear and unbelief. It will increase and multiply in the light of truth and our obedience. Talents do not only benefit the Master but also the servant to whom He has entrusted them.

Just like the talents, I believe God portions the measure or talent of faith in accordance with our ability. This measure can be increased, multiplied, buried, lost, or taken away. This measure is initially entrusted to us so we can believe that God *is,* that He exists as the Creator and Father. But if we bury the talent at this point we have limited it. Our relationship and knowledge of the Father will go no further.

With burial, the talent of faith goes into dormancy. Like a seed without soil, moisture, and pressure, it sits waiting to be planted. We cannot live on the knowledge of, "Okay, You are God." We must press on to the truth that He will reward our diligent pursuit with more knowledge and revelation of Himself.

If you only believe that God exists, you miss out on knowing Him. Or maybe you know enough to know that He *can* be a rewarder—you've seen Him do it for others but doubt He'll do it for you. This door of doubt grants entrance to fear and unbelief in your relationship with God.

God is more than just a creator and more than just a father figure. He is the Father, your Father. He is good and perfect, caring and just. So often we have only known fathers who have fallen short of perfect. But we cannot measure our heavenly Father even by the best of those on earth. We cannot even measure heaven by what we have seen.

The wicked servant knew *about* his master without ever really knowing him. He watched his actions and thought, *He is harvesting where he has not sown!* Little did he know that his master harvested where he had not sown for the benefit of those this servant had yet to see. After all, God sowed to the field of Israel yet reaped a harvest of Gentiles. God had never sown to the Gentiles; He had only judged them. How could this servant's perceptions have become so distorted?

> To the pure, all things are pure, but to those who are corrupted and do not believe, nothing is pure. In fact, both their minds and consciences are corrupted.
> —TITUS 1:15

Here is our answer. The first two servants were excited, not because they thought they were going to keep all the talents; they were excited for their master. They were glad they could give back to the one who had entrusted the talents to them. They were honored by his trust. They were pure in heart and this pureness guarded them from fear and kept them from presuming and judging their master's motives and actions.

The impurity of their fellow-servant's heart caused him to suspect the worst of his master. He judged and, in turn, later was judged. His mind or thought processes had been twisted and corrupted until even his conscience agreed with his warped reasoning and actions. What had so clouded his reason?

> See to it, brothers, that none of you has a sinful, unbelieving heart that turns away from the living God.
> —HEBREWS 3:12

Unbelief and sin cause us to *turn away* from God, only to later *turn on* Him. We will eventually turn on Him because our perception of Him is warped. How can we protect ourselves from this heart condition? We must keep our hearts pure by guarding them with the light of God's truth and purging it with the fire of God's love.

To the extent that our hearts are pure, we will see God. Don't limit this to seeing Him in heaven. We will see His truth, provision, and ways now on this earth also. When our hearts are pure, our eyes are filled with light and we see clearly.

You could never truly assess the measure of a woman without including the measure of faith. The first weight on the balance of the measure of a woman is her faith.

You are not your talents or abilities. You are not what you do. You are not your skills or inborn talents. You are not your profession or career. You are not what you do: wife, mother, career. You are not what you know: education, experience, and intelligence.

Have you ever believed God would do it for everyone else but not for you?

_____

_____

_____

What was the disappointment that led you to this conclusion? ____

_____

_____

In this situation, can you believe that God was just even if He seemed unfair? _____
_____
_____

Why are you still afraid to believe Him? _____
_____
_____
_____

I want you to stretch beyond your own talents and abilities and believe that God is good and that He can do more than you can provide. Write down an area you will turn over to Him. _____
_____
_____
_____
_____

Are you in Christ?

Then you must let go of the old.

It is gone and a new way of living has been

prepared for you. You must use your gift of faith

to step into this new life. Let go of your

past because your past is not

your future.

6

Escaping Your Past

Therefore, if anyone is in Christ, he is a new creation; the old has gone, the new has come!

—2 CORINTHIANS 5:17

ARLIER THIS year I had the honor of being one of the day-time speakers for a national conference. I had spoken the previous day and was getting ready to attend a luncheon for all the speakers before my afternoon session. I was especially excited about this opportunity to meet so many woman of God all at once! I could listen to their conversations and ask questions. On top of this, I didn't have any of my children with me. I was alone—*and* with *female adults!*

As I entered the book and tape area of the conference center and headed for the lunchroom, the Spirit arrested me:

"Go out to your car. I want to talk to you."

I felt like a child being sent to her room. Why now? Couldn't I just go in for a little while and then come outside?

I didn't sense a very positive reception from the Holy Spirit as I suggested this idea. I turned around, walked out the door I had just entered in, and returned to the vehicle I had just left.

Our ministry's big red truck was parked under the shade of a large oak tree. I climbed in a little reluctantly. There I was, in high heels and a dress, sitting in a truck in the church parking lot. By now, all the other speakers would be meeting and greeting. It reminded me of when I nursed my babies and spent most social events shut away in the confines of a back bedroom.

I decided to shake this perception of punishment. After all, one of my most treasured memories was of the peaceful faces and the sweet embraces of my nursing babies. I stilled my thoughts and listened.

Immediately I sensed God's presence. The Holy Spirit spoke to my heart as I grabbed pen and paper to scrawl down any truths He would impart. I flipped through my Bible for the references that confirmed His voice.

I don't know how long I was out there. It seemed like moments in the richness of His presence and fellowship. I didn't even want to leave when it was time for me to go inside. I am going to share with you some of the things God showed me.

That afternoon I was delivering a message called "Escaping Your Past." I had written about this subject in my first book and was pretty confident about what I would share. In the stillness of the truck, God had expanded my afternoon message.

He began by telling me that the American church has enshrined the past. The past had been set up as an excuse or justification for present behavior. When we make excuses for ourselves by drawing from our past, it is idolatry. An idol is what we give our strength to or draw our strength from.

There are those in the church who spend their strength and selves in the research of their own pasts. They study it, looking for a reason and rhyme for their life. They may think their *past* justifies their *present,* but the truth is that the *past* will never justify the *future*. This is deception. We will never change by beholding ourselves.

There are those who look intently into the mirror of their lives, hoping its reflection will hold answers for them. James describes this condition:

> Do not merely listen to the word, and so deceive yourselves. Do what it says. Anyone who listens to the word but does not do what it says is like a man who looks at his face in a mirror and, after looking at himself, goes away and immediately forgets what he looks like. But the man who looks intently into the perfect law that gives freedom, and continues to do this, not forgetting what he has heard, but doing it—he will be blessed in what he does.
> —JAMES 1:22–25

We are not the focus. Our focus is the perfect law of liberty. It will give us the freedom we now search our pasts to find. We are forgetful when we only hear the Word and do not obey it. Part of obedience is applying God's truth to our lives and circumstances. If we do not do this, we will find ourselves open to self-deception.

ACQUIRE THESE GODLY ATTRIBUTES

SECOND PETER 1:5–9 gives an outline for the healthy development of Christian attributes. First you add goodness to your measure of faith. This includes believing that God is a *good God.* Next you add knowledge to this revelation of goodness, and to knowledge, you add self-control. To this, you add perseverance; to perseverance, you add godliness; to godliness, you add brotherly kindness; and lastly, to brotherly kindness, you add love.

We are promised that if we "possess these qualities in increasing measure, they will keep you from being ineffective and unproductive in your knowledge of our Lord Jesus Christ" (2 Pet. 1:8). These are all measures that can be increased by use and the exercise of our faith.

We are also warned, "if anyone does not have them, he is near-sighted and blind, and has forgotten that he has been cleansed from his past sins" (v. 9).

Nearsighted and blind people have a hard time seeing things accurately. I know; I'm nearsighted. Without the help of my glasses, I do not recognize the form of my own husband until he is within twenty feet of me.

Impaired eyesight causes us to lose our edge and insight. The nearsighted only notice the obvious. Often the obvious over-shadows the eternal.

This shortsighted condition makes us forgetful. "Where did I leave my keys?" If the item is not right in front of us . . . we quickly forget it. Peter said this condition will cause us to forget we have been cleansed. When this knowledge is lost, we will begin to make excuses.

Why would anyone go to the trouble to explain away some-thing they were no longer accountable for? If they remembered they have been cleansed, they would simply say, "Oh, that was *before I was made new.*"

When we do not obey the truth that has been clearly revealed, we will deceive ourselves. (See James 1.) Our hearts again con-demn us if we attempt to make justification for our sins by the works of the flesh and psychology of man. Let's go back to the purpose of salvation. Was it not to restore us to God through the remission of sins and the removal of our past?

When I stand before God, I will stand alone, as an individual. Each of us is judged for what we have done. That is why I need-ed a Savior. I had lived a life that could not stand the scrutiny and presence of a holy God. I became a Christian when I experienced this revelation: I was sinful and God was holy. The two could never touch. Jesus became my Mediator.

Job described his need for a savior this way:

> If only there were someone to arbitrate between us, to lay
> his hand upon us both.
>
> —JOB 9:33

WHY WE NEED A MEDIATOR

WE HAVE THAT Someone. He mediates between God and us. Picture this: the Book of Life is opened and the written code against us is read aloud for all to hear. We cower under the weight of our sins in the presence of this holy Judge. Our sins are so gross and the list so immense and far-reaching that we tremble and fear that we are unforgivable.

Our only hope is our glorious Advocate, the Judge's only son. We weep and tremble in the silence that proceeds the pronouncement of our judgment: "You are guilty as charged." The finality and terror of this verdict grips us as an angel steps forward to escort us out.

Then our Advocate steps forward and pleads our cause. "Father, You are just to pronounce her guilty. She knew this day would come and she traded her sin-riddled life for My lordship. She has been My servant. My death satisfies the written judgment against her. The sins she has committed are under the covering of My blood."

"Forgiven," the Judge pronounces.

Now we are free! Imagine the relief and joy! Once and for eternity, we have been judged worthy of citizenship in God's kingdom—not because of what we did or the lives we lived, but because of what Jesus did. His righteousness is above question and it has been assigned to us!

Now imagine a different court scene. Again, the list of sin is read and the defendants are found guilty. Our Advocate comes before the Judge and says, "Guilty as charged, but I have shed My blood to pay her debt." This time there is one defendant who despises this extension of mercy.

She stands up and begins to justify her own actions. The Mediator rushes to her side and cautions, "If you make your own defense, I can no longer be your Mediator."

But she proceeds in her own foolish defense: "It is not my fault; you don't know what they did to me! Get my parents in here; it is *their* fault!" or, "I was hurt and rejected; that is why I

75

acted so hatefully. It is the fault of *those who hurt me!*"

The Mediator answers, "They have already been judged. They are not on trial here; *you* are."

"Well, I know I did all those things, but it was not my fault. I'll make my own defense. It's not fair!"

Though her guilt could have been blotted from God's sight, when she justified it she kept it on the record. She lost her Mediator and now stood before a breech between a holy God and her own sinful human nature.

What do you think would be this woman's sentence? She would be judged guilty, of course. Guilty of sin, unforgiveness, unbelief, and irreverence—to name a few. She would also be guilty of treating Christ's precious sacrifice as common. She would be judged, not by the mercy of the New Covenant, but by the law. For it is the law that says, "An eye for an eye." "You did this to me, so I did this to you; it's your fault."

This may seem preposterous to you, but it is not. When we excuse ourselves, we stand before God in our own righteousness. That righteousness is as filthy rags. Our defense cannot be compiled based on the reasons and motives behind what we did.

You are not justified by what was done *to* you; you are justified by what was done *for* you. You are not even justified by any good works you have done. Your sole justification is faith in Christ's sacrifice. You may be rewarded (like the faithful servants) for what you have done, but you will not be excused by it.

> Therefore, if anyone is in Christ, he is a new creation; the old has gone, the new has come!
> —2 CORINTHIANS 5:17

LETTING GO

ARE YOU IN CHRIST? Then you *must* let go of the old. It is gone and a new way of living has been prepared for you. You must use your gift of faith to step into this new life. Let go of your past because *your past is not your future.*

God is the Lord of our future. He has plans for us. He is always planning ahead so we don't have to. All we have to do is trust Him and learn His ways. His ways are higher and wiser, and He clearly tells us to forget our past.

Philippians 3:13–14 instructs us to forget what is behind. (This means *all of it*—the good, the bad, and the ugly.) It exhorts us to strain for what is ahead, loosing ourselves of the load of our past. That is the only way we can have the necessary strength to persevere to our goal.

How many marathon runners carry backpacks? If they started with one, it would soon be dropped in order to lighten their load so they could finish their race. Marathon runners compete in the lightest apparel possible and carry only what is necessary for their journey. The marathon runner knows he must conserve all his strength for the race at hand.

We also run a race. It is not only a physical race, but a spiritual one. That is what makes this race different.

> The path of the righteous is like the first gleam of dawn,
> shining ever brighter till the full light of day.
> —PROVERBS 4:18

The path becomes clearer and more distinct as we walk it. As long as we go forward, our light will increase. We can't go forward when we are looking back, so we must turn to the Son and follow His light. With each step, we leave the realm of darkness and travel deeper into His light, until it shines brighter than the full light of day.

Some of you are running with backpacks filled with stones because you are trying to bring your past into the future. Others of you are looking back. Maybe you are afraid your future will be like your past. Now is the time to put the past to rest.

When we excuse our behavior by our past, we say, "I've earned the right to be this way because of what was done to me." This attitude betrays the presence of unforgiveness in our hearts. Forgiveness is the very foundation of the gospel. Without forgiveness, there is no remission of sin. Unforgiveness will keep us bound to our past.

> Do not judge, and you will not be judged. Do not condemn, and you will not be condemned. Forgive, and you will be forgiven.
>
> —LUKE 6:37

Unforgiveness inevitably causes us to lose sight of our own need of forgiveness. We have God's promise that if we forgive, we will be forgiven. It is when we *don't forgive* that the weight of our own sins come back to bear down on us. The forgiveness of God is the very force that *releases* us from our past. We can even release others, for, "if you forgive anyone his sins, they are forgiven; if you do not forgive them, they are not forgiven" (John 20:23). But remember—by not forgiving others, we are also *not forgiven.* Some of us have withheld forgiveness as a form of punishment . . . when in the end, we are only punishing ourselves. Is it worth it?

THE POWER OF FORGIVENESS

WHEN WE WERE first married, John did something that really hurt me. It happened a few times. Each time John came to me afterward and apologized. But I would reject his apology.

"I'll believe you are sorry *when you change!*"

This response was safe for me. It meant that I did not have to extend forgiveness to John until he had proven himself worthy of it. This pattern continued for awhile. Each time John hurt me, I felt more justified in withholding my forgiveness. He would apologize and, out of my hurt, I would lash out:

"I *knew* you weren't sorry! *You did it again!* I don't even want to hear your apology!"

I was bitter and tormented because I had never extended forgiveness. It happened again; now I was mad at God *and* John. I went to prayer and asked the Lord to change my husband, and here is how the Holy Spirit answered:

"John will not be able to change *until you forgive him.*"

"I don't believe he is sorry," I argued. "If he was, he would stop it! Why is everything always my responsibility? Why do I always have to be the one to change? I'm the one who is getting hurt!"

"Tell John you believe he wants to change and that you forgive him."

God had issued some very clear directives to me without once commenting on John's behavior. I had wanted Him to judge John . . . maybe speak to him in a dream and scare the daylights out of him. God wasn't interested in my solution. Instead, He presented me with some options. Now I had the choice to obey His command to forgive and release John, or to disobey and retain his offense. I had been taught that the way you proved you were sorry was by changing.

God was challenging me to extend mercy to John when I didn't think he had earned it. That is the beauty of mercy. It cannot be earned, and it is given when we least deserve it because that is when we most need it.

I went to John and shared with him what God had told me. I apologized for punishing him with my unforgiveness. I had done it to protect myself and had wound up hurting us both. Once I was obedient, the power of God was released into our situation, and healing and restoration took place.

It was a moment of truth for me, and I would face many more. Some of them caused me to take stock of my heart, and I discovered that I didn't always like what I found there. I wanted to blame someone else. Then I would not be so uncomfortable because I would not be responsible for my own actions. Right?

I did this for awhile, hoping it would make me feel better. I had forgotten that by bringing up the past of others, I was also dredging up my own. I had forgotten that if I held my loved ones accountable for their pasts, then God would have to hold me accountable for mine. Remember, He uses the same measure and method of judgment to judge us that we have used to judge others.

We cannot pick and choose the application of scriptures to our own liking. We are quick to defend ourselves when the devil brings up our past: "That's under the blood!" or, "That person died!" If this is true—and it is—then why resurrect it?

We do it to defend ourselves. Our self-defense in the courts of earth is just as foolish as it would seem in heaven. "You know, I came from a dysfunctional family. That is why I can't help it. It's just the way I am." No, that is the way you *were* before you got saved. It is no longer the way you are to continue to live and conduct yourself. Too often we think that the abuse we suffered in the past grants us a special exception in the present. We have convinced ourselves that we do not need to change because God understands that ours is a special case, as if Jesus' death were not enough to heal and restore us. The truth is, it *was* enough—and no matter how painful your past, its hold on you was annihilated by the cross.

It is important to note that while Jesus graciously mediates on our behalf with God, He refuses to mediate between God's children. He has given us specific instructions as to how we are to treat each other and, therefore, He will not mediate our disobedience to these instructions.

Even when Jesus was on the earth, He would not mediate such disputes. "Jesus replied, 'Man, who appointed me a judge or an arbiter between you?'" (Luke 12:14). Wait a minute! Had not God appointed Him as a Judge and Arbiter? Not between God's children! Jesus was so obedient to the Father that He honored God's position as the sole Judge over His children. Though Jesus possessed the wisdom to judge righteously, He refused to do it. Instead, Jesus lived a life of perfect obedience so He could mediate on our behalf.

Jesus described His role in John 12:47: "As for the person who hears my words but does not keep them, I do not judge him. For I did not come to judge the world, but to save it." He instructed, but left it to the individual to decide whether or not they would obey His Word. Jesus was a leader, not a controller. He never *made* anyone follow Him.

What were some of His words to us?

But I tell you: Love your enemies and pray for those who persecute you, that you may be sons of your Father in heaven. He causes his sun to rise on the evil and the good, and sends rain on the righteous and the unrighteous.
—MATTHEW 5:44–45

But I tell you, Do not resist an evil person. If someone strikes you on the right cheek, turn to him the other also.
—MATTHEW 5:39

These are not the actions of people who have a past. People with pasts would say, "I tried that and it hurt me." People with pasts cannot live in the present because:

No one who puts his hand to the plow and looks back is fit for service in the kingdom of God.
—LUKE 9:62

DON'T LOOK BACK!

LOOKING BACK makes us unfit for kingdom service. We must again place our hands firmly on the plow and push forward. If we look back while we plow, our rows will be uneven and we will run the danger of breaking our plow blades on rocks or stumps. Plowing requires a constant eye fixed on what is immediately ahead in the field.

The past is gone. It is dead. We need to stop seeking the living among the dead. When we allow our focus to be diverted backward, we forget that we have been cleansed and start to make excuses.

When we look at ourselves in the mirror, we remember what manner of man *we had been* and forget what manner of man *we now are*.

Now it is time to change our focus. It is time to let go. *You are not what you have done. You are not what has been done to you. You have been translated from that dark domain onto God's path of light.*

81

Your worth is not found in *what you have done*. It is represented by *what Jesus did for you*. If you really believe what He did was enough to wash away your sins, then you must acknowledge that it was enough to wipe out your past. There are no special cases. No longer are you a woman with a past . . . you are a woman with a future.

Are you ready?

First you must release and forgive all those who have hurt you.

> *Father, forgive me for holding and retaining the sins of those who have hurt me. I realize that by imprisoning them I have imprisoned myself. I forgive them; they owe me nothing. I sow mercy because I need mercy. In Jesus' name, Amen.*

(List here or on a separate sheet those you have forgiven.)

_____
_____
_____
_____
_____
_____
_____

> *Father, forgive me for using my past to justify my present. Jesus, I embrace You as my justification and righteousness. I choose to walk in newness of life and turn my eyes off myself and onto Your Word. I will not be a hearer only. I will be a doer. Then my discernment will remain clear and accurate. I rise up out of the dust of my past. I leave behind me all the bondage of guilt and fear. From this day _____ (fill in date) forward I have no past. I will not look back at it. I go forward.*

There are certain memories and fears from your past that have crept into your present life and threaten to infiltrate the future God has planned for you. It's time to let Jesus now bury them. Let Him submerge them deep into the sea of forgetfulness. Don't speak of them anymore. Let them remain in the still silence of God's sea.

Write down the ones the Holy Spirit brings to mind once you know you have turned the past and its memories and fears over to Jesus.

_____

_____

_____

_____

_____

Now I want you to speak to these memories and fears. Tell them you are a new creation and the old is gone and no longer has any hold on you. Use your authority in God's Word and declare this truth over your life.

You have walked away from the weight and yoke of your past. Leave it behind you and turn your eyes to God's law of liberty. This will take faith and courage. God has already supplied you with a talent to do so. Unearth it and move forward.

When we look through

unveiled eyes, we will behold truth,

for He is the way, the truth, and the life.

Those who no longer fear truth

will embrace it.

7

The Unveiling

Nevertheless when one turns to the Lord, the veil is taken away.
—2 CORINTHIANS 3:16, NKJV

Y OU HAVE unearthed your talent. Now it is time to remove the veil. Something is veiled in order to conceal, mask, or cover it. Under many ancient and modern religions, women have veiled their faces and loosely draped their bodies with fabric to obscure their faces and hide their form in public. These are natural, outward masking techniques used to mute a woman's physical features and shape.

The Christian religion does not require that women veil themselves outwardly. We are often proud that we are free from the bondage of physical veiling. Yet often we are unknowingly draped in a multitude of veils.

Veils can be used deliberately to hide us from the view of others. After forty days on the mountain with God, Moses used a veil to cover the reflected radiance of his face which still shone brightly with the glory of God.

> But whenever he entered the LORD'S presence to speak with him, he removed the veil until he came out. And when he came out and told the Israelites what he had been commanded, they saw that his face was radiant. Then Moses would put the veil back over his face until he went in to speak with the LORD.
>
> —EXODUS 34:34–35

We are told that Moses' face was radiant because he had spoken with the Lord (Exod. 34:29). The Israelites recognized this radiance as the product of being in God's presence. Moses let them see the light which shined from his face while he relayed the words of God; then he draped himself. He covered God's radiance until he again met with God. In His presence, Moses unveiled his face and spoke to God face-to-face as a man would speak to his friend. His face was veiled toward man and but naked before God.

Before the sacrifice of Jesus, each of us was separated from the presence of God by a veil. The holy of holies was hidden from the sight of all mankind, except the high priest. A thick curtain separated the holy of holies from the holy place. It could only be entered by the high priest, and then only when he brought the blood for atonement.

With the death of Jesus, this heavy multi-layered and colored veil was torn asunder.

> At that moment the curtain of the temple was torn in two from top to bottom. The earth shook and the rocks split.
>
> —MATTHEW 27:51

This was a supernatural demonstration. Due to its thickness, the veil would be difficult for man to tear from bottom to top, but impossible to tear from top to bottom. Even the rocks split in two the day Jesus died.

In the beginning God instructed His people to make altars upon rocks that had been neither carved nor chiseled. After the altars of stone came the tabernacle of Moses, then the temple. By splitting stones, God rent the old order from conception to completion. The old was finished and a new and living way had begun. From the first altar of stone all the way to the rending of the temple veil, the dispensation of Moses and the law had yielded to the dispensation of the Spirit.

With the parting of the veil, the contents of the holy of holies was in clear view. Though it was unveiled, many Israelites still couldn't see.

> But their minds were made dull, for to this day the same veil remains when the old covenant is read. It has not been removed, because only in Christ is it taken away. Even to this day when Moses is read, a veil covers their hearts.
> —2 CORINTHIANS 3:14–15

THE RENDING OF THE VEIL

ONLY IN CHRIST is the veil that shrouds our hearts stripped away. The law cannot remove the veil, for the law itself had shrouded our hearts.

The reading of Moses is the reading of the law. The Israelites wanted to see, but were afraid to look. They wanted to listen, but were afraid to hear. The children of Israel came to Moses and said to him, "You talk to God for us. We don't want to talk to Him. Be our mediator, be our go-between. Tell us what He says to do and we will do it."

> When the people saw the thunder and lightning and heard the trumpet and saw the mountain in smoke, they trembled with fear. They stayed at a distance and said to Moses,

"Speak to us yourself and we will listen. But do not have God speak to us or we will die."

—EXODUS 20:18–19

This separated the Israelites from direct contact with God. They only had contact with the man, Moses, who had contact with God. Thus, the people were placed in a position to know *about* God, without really knowing Him.

You can know all about someone, yet still not recognize them if they walked right up to you. You have only heard about them and have never seen them; therefore, you do not recognize them face-to-face.

Conversely, you can visually know someone without knowing their voice. If you have never spoken with them, how could you recognize their voice if they were to call you on the phone? Only when you see them and hear them will you be able to match face and voice together.

Jesus came as Immanuel, or God with man. He was God incarnate. He could be seen, heard, spoken to, and touched. In contrast, when God descended to the mountain to speak to the Israelites, they couldn't even touch the base of the mountain of God. Violation of such boundaries meant death.

Jesus was jostled, bumped, and touched by a multitude of Israelites and some Gentiles. The fire of God did not break out and consume the people; instead, it reached out and healed them. Jesus is the union of God's Word, His holy fire, and His boundless love.

The law veils our hearts with the fear of judgment. The Israelites shook under the shadow and sound of God's law. They dared not approach Him and drew back while Moses drew near.

In contrast, the multitude pressed near to Jesus while the religious leaders drew back to plot His death. Though they had studied about Him, they did not recognize His voice nor His face. They handled Him and questioned Him, but the veil remained over their hearts and blinded their eyes. This veil was more impenetrable than the temple's.

There is only one way to remove this veil created by the fear of judgment. It is through repentance. Paul explained the spiritual significance of this rent veil:

> Nevertheless when one turns to the Lord, the veil is taken away.
> —2 CORINTHIANS 3:16, NKJV

Turning to the Lord in repentance removes—rends—the veil from our hearts. It lifts the shroud that clouds our eyes so we can clearly see truth. Before this, all we saw was blurred and void of definite form and feature. But when the veil is swept away, there is clarity. There is freedom.

> Now the Lord is the Spirit; and where the Spirit of the Lord is, there is liberty. But we all, with unveiled face, beholding as in a mirror the glory of the Lord, are being transformed into the same image from glory to glory, just as by the Spirit of the Lord.
> —2 CORINTHIANS 3:17–18, NKJV

When our faces are unveiled we can see the true image in the mirror. If we veiled ourselves and approached our own reflections, even we could not accurately see ourselves. We could only perceive the hidden portion of our features by what had been unveiled. Others could never completely be certain if behind the veil there were smiles or frowns.

Through Jesus this veil of distortion is snatched away. Our eyes then receive a portion of the revelation of God's glory. We can glimpse its radiance. As Moses, we bask in God's radiant presence. After we behold its beauty and truth, that same radiance is imparted to us and we reflect what we have received. Thus begins the transformation process from our image to His, from glory to glory.

When we look through unveiled eyes, we will behold truth, for He is the way, the truth, and the life. Those who no longer fear truth will embrace it. We will see it for what it is in the light of His mercy and grace.

Before turning to Christ the truth did not set us free; it condemned us, for when we beheld the truth, we realized we were not its reflection. We turned from its image because our own varied so vastly from it. In fear of judgment, we ran and veiled ourselves with the law or hid ourselves from God's view.

Our hearts condemned us, so we veiled our hearts, hoping to muffle and calm our fears. But our fears remained. Then we turned to Christ.

The same truth that once condemned us now brings life and liberty. Instead of judgment, we see freedom in the truth. The more we behold truth, the more we are transformed. This increases our capacity to radiate the light of God.

VEILED HEARTS

A VEILED HEART it is not hidden from God. It only obscures our vision. This causes us to believe we're unseen.

I wear glasses or contacts to correct my vision. Before I wore them, I was under the mistaken impression that no one saw me, because I could not see clearly. I would sing and bob my head in time to the music in my car, oblivious to the drivers on either side of me. If I didn't notice them, surely they didn't notice me. When I first got my glasses, I argued with the optometrist, "These are too strong! I can see everything!"

"You are supposed to," he countered.

"No, you don't understand," I insisted. "I can see leaves on the trees!"

With my former poor vision I saw a softer, blurred world. Trees were brown trunks with soft, shimmering green blobs on top. I was certain that once my vision was corrected, I would see these same images magnified, not clarified. With corrected eyesight, my world seemed smaller and less private. I noticed the people in cars, not just the cars. I wondered how often I had been waved to by people I knew, only to return their friendly greetings with a blank stares.

My eyes had been veiled by nearsighted vision. When the veil was removed, I saw clearly—sometimes more clearly than I would have wished to see. I had enjoyed the soft-focus-lens look of my face. Now in the hard light of reality, I saw every freckle and pore. Looking in the mirror one day, I asked my husband, "Is this how you see me?"

"Is *what* how I see you?" he asked, looking perplexed.

"Can you see *this?*" I asked as I pointed to a brown spot on my face.

"Yes."

"Can you see *this?*" I asked, pointing to a blemish.

"Yes."

"Have you always seen these? I don't like the way I look when I can see," I murmured as I turned from the mirror and pulled off my glasses.

John came around behind me and turned me back toward the mirror. "Do you want me to tell you what I see?"

I really did, but in response, I just shrugged my shoulders.

"Put your glasses on and look in the mirror," John ordered.

While standing behind me, he pointed out to me what he saw each time he looked at me. He highlighted all the things he liked about my features. My focus shifted from the flaws to the love that overlooked them. I looked closer for the good John saw in me.

God does the same thing with us. When we first turn from our iniquities and behold our true images, we don't like what we see. We still see the remnants of the flaws, wrinkles, and blemishes of our former lives. The clarification brings magnification to our shortcomings.

Like me with my glasses, I allowed the enemy to use my improved eyesight to point out my flaws. The flaws had always been there, and I had been loved in spite of them.

Our flaws have always been there, but God loves us in spite of them. He knows that correcting our blurred and darkened vision will cause us to accurately behold Him.

The enemy wants us to use this improved vision in a negative way to focus on ourselves. Then the Spirit encourages us to keep looking . . . *with unveiled face, beholding as in a mirror the glory of the Lord.* We don't look at ourselves with this unveiled vision; we look at the Lord.

Looking at our image does nothing to transform us . . . it simply discourages us. It limits us to ourselves. It is when we behold the glory of the Lord that we are *being transformed into the same image.*

To look deeper by the Spirit is to turn our focus from ourselves and toward Christ in us, the hope of glory. He speaks loving and comforting words to us as He patiently points us beyond the obvious, toward the glorious unseen.

Is Image Really Everything?

THE WORLD SAYS, "You are the surface; you are the image. *Image is everything!*" Well, image *is* everything to the world. The world looks in mirrors and beholds only its own veiled reflection. The world is limited to *self-image,* while we are being transformed into *God's image.*

Self-image is dependent on how you look, what you wear, what you have, whom you hang out with. It usually centers around beauty, youth, talent, and money. All of these may vary or decrease with age.

Our image as Christians does not corrode or fade with the passing of our youth. It cannot be purchased with money. It cannot be won by talents and abilities. Our image comes from beholding our Father in the face of Jesus Christ and by washing ourselves in His Word.

God does not want us to veil our faces, as Moses did. He wants us to bask in His presence and then reflect His light to others.

> Therefore, since we have such a hope, we are very bold. We are not like Moses, who would put a veil over his face to keep the Israelites from gazing at it while the radiance was fading away.
>
> —2 Corinthians 3:12–13

Since we have a hope, we are *very bold.* Moses veiled the fading radiance of the law. Though it was God-breathed and glorious, it was fleeting and temporary:

> For if what is passing away was glorious, what remains is much more glorious.
> —2 CORINTHIANS 3:11, NKJV

Under the law, the veil was all that could be seen. All that could be seen was the shroud of separation between God and man. But our gospel is much more glorious. It is uncovered for our eyes to see. It is not shrouded in a thick cloud or separated by a thick curtain. It is there for all who turn to Christ.

> And even if our gospel is veiled, it is veiled to those who are perishing. The god of this age has blinded the minds of unbelievers, so that they cannot see the light of the gospel of the glory of Christ, who is the image of God.
> —2 CORINTHIANS 4:3–4

What is the god of this age? I believe this has many facets, but the strongest is self-worship, setting *ourselves* up as god. This happens when we are self-ruled, self-seeking, self-conscious, self-serving, self-motivated and *selfish.* It is when we are the center of our universe. Those without hope live behind veils—veils of guilt, veils of fear, veils of unbelief, veils of pride, veils of religion, veils of materialism, veils of rebellion. They shroud themselves in deception in order to hide from God.

> Nothing in all creation is hidden from God's sight. Everything is uncovered and laid bare before the eyes of him to whom we must give account.
> —HEBREWS 4:13

These veils ultimately fail to shield from the piercing and penetrating truth. Each of us will either be transformed by this light or judged by it. It is not safe to hide behind the veil; when we turn to the light, we're transformed.

It is comparable to stepping out from a cold, damp, dark cellar into the warmth and vibrancy of a sunlit backyard. The spring sun there caresses you with warmth. Sitting still, you can feel the sun's radiance penetrate your clothes and warm you to the bone. A chair invites you to sit down, and you bask in the gentle warmth of sunlight until every shudder and chill from the cold cellar is gone.

When you go indoors, you see reflected in your mirror the warm glow of the sun in the heightened flush of color on your skin. People look at you and know you have been in the sun. You don't have to tell them; they recognize the glow.

It is the same with Christians. We sit in the warmth of God's presence, basking in His truth, and come away glowing and recharged. God wants us to *Son-bathe* so we can reflect His Son to others. If we *self-bathe,* no one will see His influence on us.

BE TRANSFORMED

WHEN WE TURNED to Christ all of us were unveiled, but often religion and the world will attempt to shroud us again. Unknowingly, we can allow cultural influences to drape, disfigure, and mask what God has done. These shrouds only hide our true image and worth. If we are being transformed to the image of Christ, then our worth is always increasing. Our beauty is maturing and softening. There is no reason to veil ourselves.

When we are first born again we see this radiance reflected in a gentleness and peace to replace our anxious fear of judgment and death. If we are not careful it is soon gone, and we are veiled once more. We lose the joy and boldness of our original rebirth and resign ourselves to settle with that fading reflection.

God is calling us to look at His reflection. If it is unclear and confused, then it has been shrouded in the graveclothes of religion and the works of the flesh. We need to stir ourselves to shake off the doubt that would cause us to shrink from His presence in fear of rejection.

The Lord wants to call us out of the cold, dark cellar and into the gentle warmth of the garden of the light of the knowledge of Him. Too often we are afraid to come into His presence, afraid the way will be barred by mistakes we have made since we have been Christians. We are afraid our works are not good enough or numerous enough to grant us entrance. We are afraid that if we call, He will not answer. So we hide in fear of rejection, assuming it is better not to try than to be disappointed. We don't reach out, fearing we will be turned away.

In the dark cellar of doubt, we become pale and weak. Only mushrooms and mold grow in such damp darkness. Both feed on the remains of life. This darkness is the veil of the law trying once again to separate us from God's light. The law condemns and separates. The Spirit forgives and restores. We are admonished:

> Therefore, since we have a great high priest who has gone through the heavens, Jesus the Son of God, let us hold firmly to the faith we profess. . . . Let us then approach the throne of grace with confidence, so that we may receive mercy and find grace to help us in our time of need.
> —HEBREWS 4:14, 16

We have nothing to hide. We have boldness because of Christ. He is the perfect priest. He served not as a levitical priest but as . . .

> One who has become a priest not on the basis of a regulation as to his ancestry but on the basis of the power of an indestructible life. For it is declared: "You are a priest forever, in the order of Melchizedek." The former regulation is set aside because it was weak and useless (for the law made nothing perfect), and a better hope is introduced, by which we draw near to God.
> —HEBREWS 7:16–19

God wants us unveiled and confident as we come before Him in our time of need.

Do you feel your relationship with the Lord is shrouded and cold?
_____

Are you fighting confusion over whether God accepts you when you come into His presence? _____
_____
_____

What is it that you fear He will reject? _____
_____
_____

When you go before Him, is it easier for you to behold your flaws and image, or do you see His goodness and mercy? _____
_____
_____
_____

When you look into the mirror of His perfect law of liberty, do you see His provision or your shortcomings? _____
_____
_____
_____

Was your reaction to reading the Bible different when you were first saved? _____

How did you see it then? _____
_____
_____

How do you see it now? _____
_____
_____

Has Bible reading become a religious duty? _____

*When did reading the Bible cease to be instruction, comfort, and encouragement?*_____
_____

Do you know God wants you to be transformed even more than you want to be? Do you know that He longs to speak to you more than you even want to hear from Him? He is waiting for you to turn to Him so He can remove any veils over your heart that may be separating you from glorious intimacy with Him!

Only by the
Spirit can we look beyond
the obvious and perceive
the hidden.

8

You Are Not Who They See

*The LORD does not look at the things man looks at. Man looks at
the outward appearance, but the LORD looks at the heart.*
—1 SAMUEL 16:7

WE HAVE talked about unveiling our hearts. Now let's
move to the more obvious outward veil of appearances. We are strongly influenced by what we see.
Looks can be misleading or deceptive. The outside is not a very
reliable indicator of our inward nature. Sometimes the outward
even contradicts the inward.

Only by the Spirit can we look beyond the obvious and
perceive the hidden. But even those most prophetically anointed
find it difficult to do this. Take Samuel, the founding father of

the prophetic lineage: He grew up in the temple, ministering to the Lord. God appeared repeatedly to him at Shiloh and clearly revealed Himself by the word of the Lord. This was his reputation:

> The LORD was with him and let none of his words fall to the ground. And all Israel from Dan to Beersheba knew that Samuel had been established as a prophet of the LORD.
> —1 SAMUEL 3:19–20, NKJV

Samuel was so accurate and his heart so pure that God upheld his words. God made sure that not a single one of those words fell to the ground fruitless or unfulfilled. An entire nation recognized God's hand on Samuel's life and honored him as God's mouthpiece. Samuel drew close to God, though he'd been raised up under a corrupt priesthood and disobedient leaders. He knew God's will and accurately discerned God's voice.

Yet when God sent him to anoint one of Jesse's sons, Samuel was influenced by what he saw. Samuel instructed Jesse to gather his sons.

> When they arrived, Samuel saw Eliab and thought, "Surely the LORD'S anointed stands here before the LORD." But the LORD said to Samuel, "Do not consider his appearance or his height, for I have rejected him. The LORD does not look at the things man looks at. Man looks at the outward appearance, but the LORD looks at the heart."
> —1 SAMUEL 16:6–7

A HEART AFTER GOD

AT FIRST, Samuel was certain that Jesse's firstborn, Eliab, was the Lord's anointed. He was impressed by his appearance and stature. Samuel did not see the pride hidden in his heart. In essence, God told Samuel, "Don't be swayed by what you see! Listen to My leading. I see deeper and perceive things you don't."

Eliab's appearance had won him the favor of Samuel. But God had another measure or standard—the heart.

God knew man's standard would focus on *the outward appearance*. Whether or not we like it, we are influenced by the appearance of people and things.

Let's openly discuss some of the ways the appearance of people may affect us.

THE FORCE OF FIRST IMPRESSIONS

CONSIDER WHAT happens when two professional women are introduced by a mutual friend. Both are young and attractive. They greet each other, extend hands to shake, exchange smiles, and make eye contact. Their cordial words do not betray the unspoken discourse going on in their minds.

Woman number one thinks to herself as she makes eye contact, *She is attractive, her hair looks sharp, makeup looks professional. Her lip color is a little bright, but I like her earrings.* Then she lets her eyes drop to scan her hand. *She is single, like me. She is taller, but I'm just as slender. I like her shoes and purse. I wonder what she does for a living?*

Woman number one asks out loud, "What type of business are you in?"

Woman number two has been processing information also. She has determined that woman number one is attractive, that her hair is not its natural color (but she likes it). Woman number one is shorter than her, even though her heels are higher. She notes woman number one's legs are not as thin as hers, but that she does have a good figure. She likes her suit but would like it better if it were a different color, because it washes out her face since her hair color is not natural.

Woman number two answers, "I'm a stockbroker and financial planner. How about you?"

Woman number one is impressed. That is a high-pressure position. A friendship could be to her advantage since she needs to do some financial planning.

Woman number two asks woman number one to describe her career.

"I'm an attorney with the firm of Lawson and Lawson."

Woman number two nods her respect.

A match has been made. They mutually respect each other professionally, they are both single and self-sufficient, and neither is intimidated by the looks of the other. Their assets and liabilities balance out. They can be friends. Now their conversation will turn toward things that draw them together. Now they can proceed to discuss mutual acquaintances and friends, common hobbies, and interests.

Appearance-wise, these hypothetical women were equally matched. But what happens if two very diverse women meet?

WHEN OPPOSITES DON'T ATTRACT

LET'S PAINT a different scenario: A husband and his wife, the mother of his two children, run into his old college friend and his girlfriend at the mall.

The two men are genuinely happy to see each other. They hug and assure each other, "Hey, you look *great!* How are you?"

The husband and father tells his college friend, "George, I want you to meet my wife, Beth. I don't know if you ever met at school. Honey, I knew George my junior year; we had accounting together."

The wife shakes her head and responds, "It's great to meet you, George."

Beth has been uncomfortably eyeing George's girlfriend. She already knows they are not married because she looked for a ring.

"Great to meet you, Beth! I want to introduce Lori to you. Lori, meet Brian and Beth."

"It's nice to meet you," Lori says as she smiles nervously. She feels a little awkward, like she is on approval. She did not go to school with George, Brian, or Beth and is a few years younger than them.

"Nice to meet you too," Beth answers a little coolly, as her eyes avoid direct contact with Lori's.

The two men begin to catch up as the two women awkwardly eye each other and scan the mall. Lori is all done up for a date and Beth is not. Beth doesn't like Lori. Lori is younger and thinner. She is afraid her husband might think George's girl-friend is more attractive than her. Lori is dressed in a cute shorts outfit. Beth is in a loose and comfortable maternity jumper. She'd put some weight on after her second child. She didn't think they would run into anyone they knew so she didn't wear makeup. Beth feels self-conscious.

Lori feels awkward in the silence, so she walks over to where Beth is standing off to the side and behind her husband. Before she can make any pleasant conversation, Beth fires off a question:

"How long have you known George?"

"A few years, but we have been dating only for the last few months. How long have you been married?" Lori asks.

"Six years," Beth answers smugly, then adds, "We have two children."

"Wow, that's great!" says Lori.

Beth is intimidated by Lori's warmth and good looks. She does not want to make it easy for her to feel comfortable. She turns from Lori, then reaches out and pulls on her husband's arm. It is her signal that she feels left out and wants to go on with their evening. She doesn't want to ask Lori about Lori. She wants to draw her own conclusions.

"Maybe you and George should go out to lunch sometime so you guys could catch up with each other," Beth suggests, address-ing the men and ignoring Lori.

"That would be great!" both men agree. They exchange numbers and promise to call.

The couples part and go opposite directions.

Later Brian shares with Beth his excitement about running into George and fills her in on George's professional and per-sonal achievements. Beth listens. Then Brian comments on Lori:

"I like Lori; she seems really friendly."

Beth rolls her eyes.

"Why that face?" her husband asks.

"Did you see how tight her top was? She is *friendly*, all right," Beth corrects.

"I didn't notice," Brian answers honestly.

"You know, I had a different figure before I had children," Beth asserts, wanting to disqualify Lori's attractiveness as seductive and transitory while reminding her husband of her own sacrifice.

Beth continues, "If I had all day to spend on my looks and exercise, I could look just as good as Lori! She is probably some air-head flight attendant!"

Note, the husband only said that Lori was friendly because he had seen her come over to speak to his wife. No mention or comparison were made about her attractiveness. But Beth is threatened and wants to demean Lori so she can feel better about herself. She wants to lower Lori to a level where she feels like she can compete with her. If Beth can accomplish this, then she will feel safe again.

IT BOILS DOWN TO APPEARANCE

HOW DO I know these types of conversations exist? Because I have carried them on in my mind. I have met women whom I consider different but my equal in appearance and achievement and have embraced them as friends. We can have fun together because we are different enough to be interesting but not so much as to be intimidating. I have met women I felt were much more attractive and tried to minimize their image because I was intimidated.

"John, you do understand that was not her natural hair color."

I have also known the frustration of being judged by my appearance. I have been exasperated when I felt judgment was being passed on me, reducing me to my clothing size. *I hate you! I can't believe you have four children!* This type of greeting is always said in jest . . . yet you wonder just how much truth is embedded within the humor.

I learned early on the pain of being reduced by what was seen. When I was five, I lost my right eye to cancer. The doctors gave me six months to live. They told my parents I would get a headache, go to sleep, and just not wake up. It was a very frightening time for my mother and father, who did not pass this information on to me until much later.

After my eye was removed, I wore a patch until the swelling was minimized and the socket had healed sufficiently so I could be fitted for an artificial eye.

Before this surgery, everywhere my parents took me, people would stop them and comment, "What a pretty little girl! What beautiful eyes!"

Such compliments always made me uncomfortable when I was young. I was confused because the people looked at *me*, but talked about me to my parents. I would just stand there as my mother or father collected the compliments on my behalf. Then one of my parents would inevitably respond, "What do you say?"

I'd murmur, "Thank you," while dropping my head or looking away.

I didn't care about being called pretty. To me, pretty was almost an insult. I wanted someone to say, "What an incredible tree-climber you have there!" or, "She swims like a fish!"

That was me. *Pretty* was girlish and I was an avowed *Tomboy!* I wanted to be tough and run fast. Pretty meant taking baths and washing your hair, clipping your nails, and restless nights sleeping in pincurls.

When my eye was removed, the majority of my compliments ceased. Instead, people made strange faces. They studied me from a distance, but still looked a little closer than was comfortable for me.

We lived in a small town and most everyone we had contact with knew about my eye. Most studied me with pity, then turned to talk to my mother or father as though I wasn't there. Voices would drop to a whisper: "How is she?"

"Fine," my mom would answer out loud.

Then the person would look doubtful and turn to give me a pitying smile, which I answered with a defiant glare. I wanted to yell, "I'm fine. I'm not my eye! I'm not weak; I'm still the same!"

THE CRUELTY OF JUDGING BY APPEARANCE

MY SURGERY TOOK place during the school year. The kids at school called me "one-eye" and "Cyclops." My mother had warned me not to lose face and had told me that name-calling and making fun would only increase if I cried or answered back. She encouraged me to ignore such insults and promised me her lap to cry on when I came home from school.

Many days I ran the two miles home from gradeschool while kids jeered me from the opposite side of the street. I pretended I couldn't hear them and held back my tears until I was home. My mother held me and told me kids this age were cruel, assuring me that when I grew up it would not be like this.

The name-calling did stop, but not the measuring of individuals by outward appearance. We have all grown up and most of us no longer play the cruel and obvious game of name-calling with our peers. We know that would be blatant judging. But what about more subtle prejudices?

You are not what you see. You are not what they see. So they are not what you see.

The little five-year-old girl in me knew I was not the way I was perceived. At five, I fought against the concept that I could be measured by how I looked, but later in life I embraced this shallow standard.

As children we are not immediately indoctrinated by cultural influences. These forces take some time to mold the metal of our souls. But once the metal is forged, it cools quickly into a hard, rigid standard by which we continually measure ourselves and others.

It is not long before little girls can't wait to be grown-ups. They long to adorn themselves in the outward accessories of makeup and jewelry. They play dress-up and put on cosmetics when they are possibly at their prettiest. Soon they are teens and they dabble daily in what was once only play. They begin to think they are not pretty without makeup, and what was once reserved for special occasions becomes a daily mandatory ritual. They want to look and act older.

Then something dreadful happens. They finally reach the age they had longed to achieve and now they are bothered with the worry of getting old. If sixteen to twenty-six is the optimum age range, it is a very short time in the whole scheme of life. As young women approach thirty, they no longer want to look older—they want to look *younger!*

This is a no-win situation for women. Men don't seem to wrestle with their age quite as much. Their maturing process is more normal. They want to grow up and become independent, but then they don't wig out because they look older! Some women even lie about their age or go to great lengths to hide it. Not content to look great at their real age, they want to appear younger and wiser. Youth and wisdom do not often pair themselves. Wisdom comes with time, obedience, and application of truth. Often we do not have access to these insights until we are old enough to appreciate their importance.

A PRECIOUS ADORNMENT

YOUNG WOMEN make the mistake of putting their trust in their face or form while neglecting their incorruptible assets. We all know the verse in 1 Peter:

> Do not let your adornment be merely outward—arranging the hair, wearing gold, or putting on fine apparel—rather let it be the hidden person of the heart, with the incorruptible beauty of a gentle and quiet spirit, which is very precious in the sight of God.
>
> —1 PETER 3:3–4, NKJV

God admonishes us to not allow our adornment to be merely outward or superficial. He is not telling us to not adorn ourselves, but that the emphasis of our adornment should be on the inside, not the outside. God is not advocating the neglect of our hair, the wearing of rags, and the absence of jewelry.

Remember, God's focus is not on the outward appearance;

ours is. He doesn't judge the way we do. He judges not what is seen, but the unseen condition of the heart. He warns us not to spend ourselves adorning what will not count for eternity. He wants us to adorn our hearts with His unfading, quiet, and gentle beauty. It doesn't age, it can't be stolen, and doesn't turn gray.

Because God's perspective is eternity, He is letting us in on His secret beauty prescription. It is an intimate beauty, one reserved for the eyes of God. It is a kind of beauty others may not notice. But God does.

When you have that inner peace and rest, the world will notice it more than your newest designer outfit, hair color, or jewelry. Those in the world have all those things, but what they don't have is peace, "which is of great worth in God's sight" (1 Pet. 3:4).

Those in the world have a confused standard for value and worth. They drape themselves to hide their emptiness while we purify ourselves to gain transparency. They hide while we shine. Unfortunately, we have allowed the marketing of the world's illusions to influence our outward projections and veil our inward reflection.

JUDGING OR MISJUDGING?

BECAUSE WE have judged by appearances, we often misjudge. Adornment is like a bowl that holds fruit, one that could be displayed on the dining-room table. It is beautifully crafted and forged of cut crystal, yet holds in its beauty fruit that is artificial and tasteless. The fruit may look initially inviting because it is surrounded by outward beauty, but if handled or sampled, the fruit will soon be revealed as worthless.

Somewhere in the pantry there is a worn and tattered crate that holds real produce. It is not beautiful yet bears what is delicious, fresh, and life-giving. If you were hungry—hungry for truth, hungry for the real—you'd turn from the beauty of the cut crystal bowl filled with artificial fruit and head for the useful, fruitful crate.

God judges us by our *fruit*, not our *fruit bowls*. He wants our inner adornment to be fresh and useful, not cold, beautiful, yet artificial. Therefore, we are mistaken when we judge others by the packaging of outward appearances.

How often are you intimidated by what you see outwardly in others?

_____

Have you whittled them down until you were no longer intimidated by them? _____

*What intimidates you the most about other women (weight, beauty, career, marital status, etc.)?*_____

_____

Have you been judged by your appearance? _____

Was it frustrating? _____

Do you draw your confidence from the outward or the inward? _____

_____

Which do you spend more time and thought on? _____

> *Father, I repent of allowing outward appearances to affect my perceptions and relationships with others. Forgive me for comparisons and competition. You never compare us with others. Remove the cultural influences that distort my vision. In the next few chapters, give me eyes to see. Amen.*

I measured
myself by the scales,
determining that I was
worthy of love if I was thin
but not if I was fat.

9

You Are Not What You Weigh

Is not life more important than food, and the body more important than clothes?

—*MATTHEW 6:25*

THOUGH YOU may be worth your weight in gold . . . you are not what you weigh! Too many of us measure ourselves by numbers on the scale instead of by the treasury of the heart. This chapter is especially pertinent, since we live in a society that says, *"You can never be too rich or too thin!"* Neither is true.

I was leaving in a few weeks to do a women's retreat in Arizona. I had been forwarded a copy of the schedule along with a brochure. I was scheduled to fly out Thursday and arrive late that evening, then leave the next morning for the remote retreat center. I would be accompanied by my infant son. As the keynote speaker, I was scheduled to minister Friday and Saturday evenings and Sunday morning. I liked this schedule because it wasn't too heavy for a jet-lagged nursing mother.

The brochure had listed some special-interest workshops scheduled for Saturday at 10:00 A.M. I had glanced at the titles and subjects when the Holy Spirit prompted me, "I want you to do a workshop on weight."

"I've never preached on weight," I argued.

I looked again at the list of topics and noticed that they were all spiritual and deep. I thought, *They will think I am carnal! They'll want to cancel me. I wouldn't even know what to call it.*

"Call it *Weighed Down by Weight,*" the Holy Spirit answered. "If it holds my people in bondage, preaching on weight is not *carnal* but *liberating.*"

The impression became stronger. With the conference just a few weeks away, I felt certain that it would be too late to add another session, but in obedience I called the pastor's wife. Even though I felt silly, I offered to do a workshop in conjunction with the 10:00 A.M. sessions. The pastor's wife said she wasn't sure if that would work out. (I secretly hoped it wouldn't.) When I did not hear back from her, I assumed it had not.

BREAKING THE BONDAGE OF WEIGHT

THERE WERE over a hundred women gathered at the retreat. They had prayed and set this time apart for fellowship with the Father. There was such a sense of expectancy that I was excited to begin the meetings. Friday night there was such liberty in the worship and praise that I hardly wanted to minister. We had a glorious service that night that extended past midnight. At the close of the service, I looked at the pastor's wife and told her I was glad the additional session had not worked out.

She appeared to be surprised and explained, "I forgot to tell you. We had to move the workshop on weight to 2:00 P.M. There were too many women registered for it to do it conjunction with any of the other sessions."

"How many registered?" I asked.

"Oh, about ninety," she answered.

I tried to hide my shock. I was totally unprepared. I returned to my room exhausted, nursed my little one, and went to bed. I tossed and turned all night in a restless sleep.

The next morning I prayed, "Father, I don't know what to say to them!"

He gave me a few scriptures and told me to share my testimony of how I had once been in bondage to anorexia. The scripture verse He gave me was:

> Therefore I tell you, do not worry about your life, what you will eat or drink; or about your body, what you will wear. Is not life more important than food, and the body more important than clothes?
>
> —MATTHEW 6:25

Worrying is taking thought. When we worry or fret about something, it is always disruptive and destructive to our peace of mind. Worry is never constructive and is always accompanied by fear and torment. Worry can become self-consuming. We could rephrase this scripture by changing the phrase "do not worry" to "think about obsessively." This verse would then read:

> Therefore I tell you, do not think obsessively about your life, what you will eat or drink; or about your body, what you will wear. Is not life more important than food, and the body more important than clothes?
>
> —MATTHEW 6:25, author paraphrase

MY OWN OBSESSION WITH WEIGHT

THERE WAS a time when my weight was all I thought about. I want to take you back to that time. Perhaps you will recognize someone you know and love in my story. Maybe you will even glimpse a reflection of yourself in my words. My struggle with weight began before I was a Christian but continued after I had become one. I know many women who wrestle with this. It is important to God and a living part of my testimony.

Until I was sixteen I had no awareness of my body weight. I was only weighed at summer camp to make certain I wasn't losing weight and at physicals to determine growth. Until then I perceived increases in my weight the same way I viewed increases in my height—as a sign I was maturing.

I was always very active and swam nearly year round on one swim team or another. I was young and active. I ate whatever I wanted, whenever I wanted, without a thought about my weight.

My junior year, I ran hurdles and pulled my Achilles' tendon while in training. I was on crutches for awhile and decided not to swim so that my ankle would heal. My activity level decreased, but I still ate as though I were in training.

One day as I walked in from school, my father stopped me and looked me over disapprovingly.

"Turn around," he said. "Boy, those jeans are tight! How much do you weigh?"

"One hundred twenty-eight," I answered, giving my camp weight from the previous summer.

"There is *no way* you weigh that! You're at least one hundred and thirty-five!" he challenged and then ordered, "Go weigh yourself!"

I wandered into my parents' bathroom and stepped onto their scale. To my disbelief, I weighed one hundred thirty-eight!

Ashamed, I reported my weight to my father. He told me I was much too big. I went in to my room and looked at myself—really looked at my body—for the first time. I pulled off my jeans. They were too tight! I could see all the seam lines and in some places even the stitches running up and down my legs. I changed into looser clothes and went over to my closet. What else was too tight? I began to pull my clothes out and try on different things. "You're fat!" I chided as I stared at my reflection in the mirror.

That night under the watchful eye of my father, I denied myself seconds and dessert. After dinner I pulled on my swimming sweats and a down coat and ran the snowdrifts until I felt as though my lungs would tear from exposure to the cold winter air. I was determined to lose the weight and get back to my weight of one hundred and twenty-eight. The next day at lunch I ate only a Big Mac and fries instead of my normal Big Mac, fries, cheeseburger, and Snickers bar. At dinner each night I cut back my portions and after dinner I ran. I pored over articles in my mother's magazines that gave information on weight loss and dieting.

In two weeks I had lost ten pounds. Everyone at school noticed. Even some of the upperclassmen complimented my weight loss. I felt powerful. I had conquered my body. I was in charge of my weight. *I would never be fat again!* I swam again my senior year and grew another inch to five-foot-seven. My weight whittled down to a muscular one hundred twenty-five.

SORORITY SISTERS

I WENT FAR from my home state of Indiana for college. I wanted to be far away from all that was familiar. I wanted to experience the West, so I traveled to the University of Arizona. I went through sorority rush and pledged a house before school had even started. Now I had friends.

I couldn't help but notice that all the girls were tan, thin, beautiful, and that the majority of them were blonde. Suddenly I felt awkward and clumsy among these svelte Barbie-lookalikes in designer jeans and ponytails. In comparison with my newly acquired California and Arizona sorority sisters, my one-hundred-twenty-five-pound body looked like an Indiana corn-fed heifer. I tried not to draw the comparison, but it was everywhere I looked.

At dinner girls thinner than myself would complain, "I'm so fat! Look at these thighs!"

I would, and I realized theirs were smaller than mine. If these girls were fat, then I was *obese!*

"How much do you weigh?" I asked the girl who had just complained of having fat thighs.

"One hundred and fifteen."

"Oh, you're thin. You're not fat!" I protested.

The girl jumped up from the table, grabbed the back of her thigh, and squeezed it. "Look at all this cottage cheese! I am *too* fat."

I felt foolish. I could only see fat because she had grabbed her thigh in a vice grip. I remained silent as I scooted further in under the table and prayed no one would ask my weight. I was ten pounds heavier than she. It had never crossed my mind that I was also three inches taller.

That night in the privacy of my dorm room I checked my own thighs. *There it was! I had it too!* Maybe she had been hinting about fat thighs so I would lose weight.

I began to run again. I stopped eating the sandwiches at lunch and would only eat the salad. My weight dropped to one hundred and twelve. But still I did not feel thin enough.

At every meal my sorority sisters and I discussed the caloric count of each item on our plates. The one who knew the most about dieting was considered to be smartest. We ruthlessly confessed and pointed out our flaws to each other: "Look at my stomach! Isn't it disgusting?" we'd complain as we lifted our shirts for inspection.

"Well, look at this!" another girl would counter, pinching young, taunt, tan legs, looking for a flaw.

My stomach was flat, my thighs were tan and thin, my arms were muscular and trim, *but I had a flaw.*

Mine was my face. Each time I looked in the mirror, I saw failure there. My jaw is square and no matter how thin I get, it will always look wide. I would stare in the mirror and all I could see staring back at me was a huge face. I would critically assess myself as though I were my own worst enemy: "I'll get rid of these jowls!" I would vow as I grabbed my lower cheeks.

At one point during my junior year, I wore a size one and weighed one hundred and three pounds. And still my face looked fat whenever I looked in the mirror. It was all I could see. My focus was so distorted that I didn't notice the gauntness there or the veins that laced my neck.

When I went home for Christmas my mother was alarmed by how much weight I had lost. She was so concerned that she took me to the doctor. He assured her that I was still within the safety limits for my height. When my mother left the room, he asked me if I had tried to lose the weight.

"No, it is just too hot to eat," I assured him.

This was a partial truth. Arizona was considerably hotter and heavy foods did seem uncomfortable.

"Well, just make sure you take care of yourself," he warned. "Maybe you should get up in the middle of the night and eat a steak!"

I smiled, though the very thought of eating steak revolted me, and I finished getting dressed.

That night my mother made my favorite meal.

"I'm not hungry," I told her.

"You have to eat!" she insisted.

"I'll eat later with my friends. I'm going out to a party tonight. We'll get pizza after."

"You need something healthy. You've hardly eaten all day!"

FOOD, MY ENEMY

SHE WAS RIGHT. I had hardly eaten. I was afraid that by coming home, I would get fat again. I thought everyone was trying to force food on me. *They don't want me thin,* I thought. *They're against me.*

My mom even tried to enlist my father's support. "Joe, tell her to eat."

"She'll be fine," he assured as he looked up from his paper and smiled at me. I knew my new weight had won his approval. At least he wouldn't push me to eat!

I went out that night with my new, improved, tanned, Arizona body. I felt like a different person. I walked and talked like my

117

sorority sisters. I had learned something else from them, too—how to party! I flitted around the party, drawing strength from this newfound attention.

"You look great! I should have asked *you* to the prom!"

Wow, was all this real, or was it a dream? Boys who had never given me a second glance in high school were now asking me out. As I lay in bed that night I determined never to go back to what I had weighed before.

But when I returned to school I realized that I had gained some of my weight back. While complaining to a sorority sister about it, she suggested that I start taking water-retention pills. I remembered my mother had taken them, but I wasn't sure what the pills were for.

"Isn't that just for before your period?" I asked.

"No!" she assured me. "I take them every Friday morning so I'll be *thin* by Friday night!"

It sounded too good to be true.

"Are you sure the pills are okay?"

"Yes, look—they are not even prescription!"

She handed me a box of over-the-counter water pills. They looked harmless. I flipped the package over and read the ingredients.

"It's got a lot of caffeine in it."

"Yeah, it's great—it gives you a buzz! Try one."

I put one of the pills in my pocket. I'd always been able to lose weight easily before. I'd lose it again.

But this time the weight loss took longer. Meals were getting harder for me to resist. In addition to the calorie counts and diet tips, my sorority sisters and I all shared a love-hate relationship with food. Food was our enemy *because it made us fat*, but we loved it *because it tasted so good!*

Food began to hold a different place in my life. I began to think about it more and more. I developed a passion for it and for drinking. I loved everything to the extreme. If I drank, I drank to get drunk. If I ate, I ate until I was uncomfortable. But I still wanted to get attention for my looks, so I exercised to the extreme. I ate excessively or dieted excessively. There was no in-between. I only thought about school when I had a test and still managed to retain a B average.

The law of food restriction had aroused in me an excessive desire for it. The law will always eventually enflame the passions of the flesh and soul. I could starve myself, but once I started to eat again, there was no stopping until I physically could eat no more. It was either feast or famine.

GOING TO EXTREMES

THIS WAS a hard lifestyle to maintain, so I enlisted the help of laxatives and diuretics in my battle. By my junior year in college my body had become addicted to them. It no longer functioned normally. Coupled with a stomach disorder I had already, I was in constant discomfort. I was afraid of my own body. What if I got fat? What if I couldn't go to the bathroom?

I became ill and ran a constant low-grade fever. A rash broke out all over my upper body. I went by the school infirmary.

"How long has it been since your last bowel movement?" the doctor asked, looking concerned as she poked my stomach.

"A month. But usually I go once a week," I assured her.

The doctor shook her head in disbelief. "Honey, you should go every day. We are going to have to do some tests on you."

First I was x-rayed. I was told that my intestines were backed up to my lungs. I was immediately checked into the hospital under the care of a specialist. It was a nightmare. I was given a prescription-strength laxative, and when that didn't work, I was given a tumbler full of castor oil to drink. The cramping was horrible. Then I went through a series of tests and was diagnosed with irritable bowel syndrome and severe lactose intolerance. The whole ordeal shook me enough so that I stopped taking laxatives and diuretics. But I was still obsessed with my weight.

At dinner one evening I watched one of my sorority sisters eat. She consumed everything on her plate and then some. And she wasn't fat. How did she do it? I never saw her running or exercising. In private, I asked her the secret.

"I eat everything I want; then I go in the bathroom and stick my toothbrush handle down my throat. Then I brush my teeth."

"Can you show me how?" I asked.

"Sure; after dinner tonight just come and brush your teeth with me."

That night after dinner I followed her ponytailed form upstairs to our common bathroom. For the first time I noticed a lot of my sorority sisters walking into the stalls with toothbrushes in hand.

"Just go in and do it."

THE ULTIMATE DIET

I HESITATED. I hated throwing up. I had even known of someone who had died by choking or by breathing their vomit. Did I really want to do this?

My thin sorority sister smiled and shrugged at me as if to say, *Whatever.* Then she slipped into the privacy of her stall. I listened. It didn't really sound like she was throwing up; only choking a little.

"Did you?"

"Yes, it is that easy."

I bravely stepped into my stall and knelt down in front of the toilet bowl. Before this, I had only knelt when I prayed. Now I was kneeling before a toilet. I jumped to my feet.

"I can't do it," I protested.

"*Sure,* you can. I do it all the time," she encouraged me with the voice of a cheerleader. I closed my eyes and pushed the toothbrush handle toward the back of my throat. I gagged.

"It didn't work!"

"Try again."

I gagged again. My eyes began to water in reflex to my gagging. I stood up. *I can't do this. I'll just have to starve myself or think of something else!* The school year was almost over and I was still thinner than most of the girls back home in Indiana. I'd figure something out that summer.

That summer proved to be very different from all the other summer breaks I'd had. That summer, I heard the gospel for the first time and I became a Christian. Jesus filled a void in me that I had tried to fill with attention from boys. I began to relax, realizing that God loved me just the way I was. I stopped my excessive exercising, dieting, and drinking, and began to look healthy again.

Christians may not drink, but they love to eat. Now every social event I attended centered around food! At church picnics, we ate; after church, we ate; on dates, we ate. The only problem was my excessive tendencies had now translated into increased consumption of food.

Around these bountiful Christian tables no one talked about calories or the vices of food. Food was a celebration. I celebrated with everyone else and soon I had put back on most the weight I had lost.

I got engaged and needed to return home to Indiana to make the wedding preparations. I was a little overweight . . . but John didn't seem to notice it.

In August of 1982 I was back up to one hundred twenty-eight pounds, but it was no longer muscle weight. I had two months before my wedding and decided I would just have to exercise and get back in shape while I was home. But home was filled with turmoil. I responded to this turmoil by eating.

If I was bored I would walk over to the refrigerator and even if I wasn't hungry, I would open the door and look in. I began to binge or starve myself.

My days consisted of getting up, weighing myself, eating breakfast, weighing myself, running errands, eating lunch, weighing myself, making phone calls and other wedding arrangements, eating dinner, weighing myself, getting discouraged, and binge-eating!

I would binge and promise myself I could eat everything I wanted to eat now, because the next day I would not eat at all! I would eat until it was painful, then I would go to sleep and have nightmares that I had eaten everything in the refrigerator. I would wake up in a sweat and reassure myself that I had not!

UPS AND DOWNS

THE NEXT DAY I might not eat at all, but I thought about food all day. *How good it would taste!* I would open and close the refrigerator. I would look into the freezer. I would weigh myself upon rising and again in the afternoon and evening. Often I would not even lose a pound! Discouraged, I would go on the eating binge again. I tried liquid diets and high-protein ones but they all failed. My parents had separated. All my friends were out of town. I felt fat and ugly. I was missing John.

Then came the day of reckoning. It was four weeks until my wedding. I needed to rent a slip for my size-nine wedding gown. I brought my wedding dress so we could determine the appropriate slip size. My gown buttoned almost entirely down the back. I stepped into and pushed the sides together so the sales clerk could button it.

"Honey, there must be a mistake!" she exclaimed.

"What do you mean?" I questioned.

"This must not be your gown! There is *no way* you can fit into this! The buttons are this far apart!" she exclaimed as she gestured with her finger and thumb a span of three to four inches.

"Here, it was a little tight; let me push it in," I said, as I sucked in my stomach and pinched in my waist.

"Sweetheart, there has been a mistake! This could not be your gown. I still can't close it. The buttons will tear off."

I could feel my face flushing with embarrassment.

"Just get me the slip and I'll try it on without buttoning it," I said.

"Okay," she said as she walked out of the fitting room, shaking her head and muttering.

Surely the sales assistant was exaggerating! As soon as she was gone, I whirled around, contorting myself in order to see the back of my gown. To my horror, she was right. It was impossible to even make the sides meet, let alone button them. In the last month, I had outgrown my wedding gown.

I placed an order for a slip, gathered my gown, and raced

home. The gown had been just a little tight when I bought it. I had been certain I would lose weight at home, not gain it like I had. I never dreamed this would happen! My parents had spent a lot of money on this gown. Now I wondered if I'd ever wear it.

I got home and ran straight upstairs to my room. I grabbed my Bible and threw myself down on the hardwood floors. I didn't want the comfort of my bed. I wanted reality to settle in. I cried and poured my heart out before the Lord.

GOD'S ANSWER

"GOD, HOW could You allow this to happen? I don't eat all day and still do not lose a pound. I can only eat an apple and a yogurt and gain one pound. I can binge and gain two pounds overnight! I'm tired of trying and failing. Why can't I eat normally?"

I wept some more as I thought of my father's and mother's faces when I would tell them the news of my dress. I felt overwhelmed and sorry for myself. When I had spent myself with crying, a quiet settled over me. I heard a still, small voice speak to me.

"Lisa, your weight is an idol to you."

An idol! All I could envision was the picture of a golden calf from my illustrated Bible. But I remained quiet and listened.

"Whenever you are lonely, you eat. Whenever you are angry, you eat. Whenever you are bored, you eat. Whenever you are depressed, you eat. Whenever you are happy, you eat."

That about covered it.

"You do not come to Me. You do not read My Word. You eat, because it is easier."

Every time I tried to read my Bible, the oppression in our house was so strong I would fall asleep. Yet I could watch TV for hours and remain wide awake. The same thing happened when I tried to pray.

The still, small voice continued: "You feel good about yourself when you are thin and bad about yourself when you are fat. You are not Spirit-led; your weight controls your moods and your life. It is an idol to you."

I saw it! It was all true. Food had dominated my thought life and even tormented my rest. I had not even shared my faith because I felt I would be rejected because I was fat. I began to cry tears of repentance.

I saw how I had drawn strength from my weight and not from God. I measured myself by the scales, determining that I was worthy of love if I was thin but not if I was fat.

"If you will repent, I will heal your metabolism. Do not diet and do not weigh yourself. Separate yourself and fast for three days on juices and water, and I will rid your body of its cravings. I will teach you how to eat again. Write down the weight you should be and put it in your Bible."

I no longer had any idea what my weight should be. I weighed over one hundred and thirty pounds at the time.

"God, You made me. What should I weigh?" My perceptions were so warped, I knew I would pick a weight far too light for my tall but petite frame. I got real quiet and as I listened, a figure floated into my head. I scribbled the number down and tucked the paper into my Bible. It was more than my former anorexic one hundred and three pounds. I thought I should weigh one hundred and ten but wrote down anther figure.

I got up from the floor and grabbed the scales. I climbed high atop a bedroom chair and placed them in the attic access in my bedroom closet. God had told me not to weigh myself. In order to weigh myself, I would have to climb up there to get at the scales, all the while knowing I was disobeying God.

FASTING TO BREAK YOKES

I WENT INTO my bathroom and splashed the tears from my face. I headed straight for the grocery store. As I walked down the juice aisle, I sensed so strongly God leading me to buy two quarts of unfiltered organic apple-strawberry juice and a couple of gallons of purified water. I had never had unfiltered juice before. The next day would begin a new way of life for me. I was not fasting to lose weight; I was fasting to fellowship with God.

My focus was not weight loss. I had sensed God's presence and leading in this fast. I had sensed His pleasure with me for repenting and choosing to fast in order to draw closer to Him. For the next three days, I drank apple-strawberry juice, straight or diluted, or just purified water. God sustained me since He had called me to the fast. I went for walks and talked with Him. I listened to praise and worship tapes and wept in His presence.

Then the fast of food was over. It was time for me to learn a fasted lifestyle. I would eat until I was satisfied, not until I was engorged. Because I had never known the difference before, praying before eating took on a whole new meaning for me. At mealtime, I would offer up my food with thanksgiving. I thanked God that food was not my enemy nor was it my satisfaction. It would bring strength to my body and I, in turn, would worship God. Fear would hit me: "If you eat that food, you'll get fat! Starve yourself." Or gluttony would attempt to entice me: "That tasted good; you need to eat more!"

I was determined not to eat simply because food tasted good, but to eat because I was feeding myself. I refused to be mastered by my passions any longer. I would inwardly listen and know when I was satisfied. I would then put my fork down and not eat another bite.

I was so excited at what God was showing me, and so happy to be developing this sensitivity that I always wanted to obey. Even when my loved ones tried to encourage me to have more, I would say, "No, thank you! I am satisfied!"

I felt great! I would walk a mile each night and pray and talk to God. I would not run to burn calories; instead, I would just walk and talk to God. I knew I was losing weight but decided not even to notice it.

My wedding was now just a few days away and I had lived like this for over three weeks. I had no idea how much I weighed; nor was I interested. However, I did need to know that my wedding dress would fit. I tried it on. Not only did it fit, it hung a little loose. I laughed with joy! I would be able to wear my beautiful dress.

My wedding was wonderful, and when I came home to change

into my going-away outfit, God stopped me and said, *"Now* you can weigh yourself."

I got the scales down and stepped on them. The needle teetered between one hundred and ten and one hundred and twenty. I jumped off the scale and grabbed my Bible. Flipping through it, I found the slip of paper with the number scrawled on it. I had forgotten the number I had written down four weeks earlier. I looked down and read—one hundred sixteen pounds. I jumped back on the scales in disbelief; it was my *exact weight!* I knew that God had healed my body. He had formed me in my mother's womb . . . and He could heal me.

FREEDOM IN CHRIST

NO LONGER was I interested in pleasing everyone else. I wanted to please God. He has told us that He knows what we need even before we ask. He has told us that we are fearfully and wonderfully made. He does not measure us by the seen but by the unseen. This scripture took on a whole new meaning to me:

> Therefore I tell you, do not worry about your life, what you will eat or drink; or about your body, what you will wear. Is not life more important than food, and the body more important than clothes?
>
> —MATTHEW 6:25

Thinking about these material things is a waste of time! Jesus admonishes us that worrying can't add even an inch to our stature. He called that a simple thing. He said if we can't change the small and simple, it is useless to worry about the big things.

When fear and worry came to torment me—"What is going to happen when you have children?" "What if you can't lose the weight?"—I fought back with the Word, not my own experience. I would counter that God would perfect that which concerned me and that children were a blessing of the Lord. I refused to believe that having children would destroy me physically. I have four, and they have periodically taxed my strength and back, but I still use the Word of God to control my figure.

When you worry about your weight, it changes your metabolism. It is a proven fact that fear and worry can influence your digestive and metabolic system.

I relaxed, nursed my children, and enjoyed them without worrying about exercising back down to my pre-pregnancy size. With each of them, I went back to my same size or smaller.

God has been faithful to keep me at that weight independent of diet and exercise. I have trusted Him to watch over my weight as long as I keep food in its proper place. I eat until I am satisfied. When I am at home, I eat healthy because I want to take care of myself, not for weight loss purposes. When it is time to celebrate, I enjoy food. But I eat to celebrate . . . not celebrate eating.

This chapter isn't about losing weight; it's about what you put your trust in. It is about how you spend yourself. I, too, was weighed down by weight until I humbled myself with fasting and God healed me.

❧

Did you see yourself in this chapter? _____

Does food meet needs in your life that only God can meet? _____

_____

What are some of those needs? _____

_____

_____

_____

_____

Are these needs really being met, or are you still dissatisfied? _____

_____

Is food an idol in your life? _____

Do you allow your weight to dictate your moods? _____

Do you feel good about yourself only when you are thin? _____

_____

Do you feel bad about yourself when your weight fluctuates? _____

_____

What is controlling you? _____

_____

_____

_____

_____

You are not what you weigh. Are you ready to leave this fallacy behind and move on? _____

If you are serious, pray with me:

> *Father God, forgive me for allowing food and my weight to hold the wrong place in my life. I repent of idolatry. No longer will I measure myself by the scales. No longer will I count calories and diet. I will offer up my food with prayer and thanksgiving and trust You to show me when I have had enough to eat. I will eat because You have provided food for my nourishment.*
>
> *I will no longer be ruled by my stomach. I will no longer worry and fret over my weight . . . I will trust You. Heal my metabolism. I will no longer speak curses over my body; instead, I will speak the truth of Your Word.*
>
> *I will not abuse laxatives and diuretics. Lord, rebalance every area of my body. Since You formed me, show me what I should*

weigh and how I should eat. Speak my ideal weight to me and I will write it down. I turn this entire area of my life over to You. Take total control of it.

Date: _____

Signature: _____

From this day forward, this is an area where you are to take no thought or measure for yourself. Do not take it back.

The fast

I refer to is not for weight

gain or loss. . . . It is not designed

to change the way we look and feel,

but to change the way we

perceive and live.

10

Fasting

Is not this the kind of fasting I have chosen: to loose the chains of injustice and untie the cords of the yoke, to set the oppressed free and break every yoke? Is it not to share your food with the hungry and to provide the poor wanderer with shelter—when you see the naked, to clothe him, and not to turn away from your own flesh and blood?

—ISAIAH 58:6–7

GOD TOLD ME *not* to diet; then He told me *to fast.* This would seem a contradiction, since both involve a restriction of food. The difference lies in the purpose or motive that inspires them. A diet is designed to lose weight or gain it. A change of diet also may be taken to improve or correct health problems. Diet is a natural application that alters our physical weight or health. It changes the way we *look* or *feel.*

The fast I refer to is not for weight gain or loss. Nor is it applied for natural healing. It is not designed to change the way we look and feel, but to change the way we *perceive* and *live.* The world has perverted the fast and diminished it to a diet. But if

131

fasting is confused with dieting, it is then not a spiritual renewal but a physical one.

Before my confrontation with truth, I had only fasted to lose weight. I might have done a combination fast, because my reasoning went something like this: *I need to lose weight and I need to pray, so I'll fast and accomplish both.* But on these types of fasts, food and weight were still the focal points. Nowhere in God's Word is a fast prescribed for weight loss. Our focus on a fast will be our reward. If God isn't the center, the fast will be reduced to merely a denial of food or pleasure.

The fast I described in the earlier chapter was not about food. It was about *faith.* I had put my faith in my weight. The fast transferred my dependence from food to God. I wanted to know Him. I wanted His truth in my innermost being. *I wanted transformation, not just weight reduction.*

For too long I had measured myself by my bathroom scales, allowing them to dictate my moods and actions. I was not Spirit-led, I was weight-led. *I was weighed down by weight.* The fast was not the turning point for my weight loss; it was the turning point of my faith. I had trusted in myself only to be disappointed again and again. I needed a complete spiritual and an emotional overhaul. When I saw my idolatry . . .

> I wept and chastened my soul with fasting.
> —PSALM 69:10, NKJV

Notice David chastened his soul. It was my soul that had risen up and given my weight preeminence. My soul had confused *slim* with *success.* My soul had longed for my father's approval and for the approval of men. My soul had distorted my vision and perception until I had no other focus but my physical size, shape, and weight. I had allowed my soul to lead me away from truth and moderation. My soul had to be chastened. I had to rise up in the Spirit and subject my soul to a chastening fast.

Some definitions of the word *chasten* are "to discipline, purify, refine, clarify, and improve." *Discipline* means "training." My soul had to be retrained, reprogrammed. Chastening was necessary to educate and cultivate a new "me." This chastening by fasting began a purification, clarification, and refinement of my soul and motives. The clarification process brought insight so that I could see clearly. Just as parents discipline their children to help them grow and learn right from wrong, my soul had to be chastened by the Lord so that I could improve and become wiser.

This refinement of my soul worked its way out and overtook my natural body and appetites which were refined and purified by the denial of food. Once the cravings of my soul were mastered, the cravings of my flesh were mastered also. I was no longer enflamed with a passion for food. My body had been denied salt and sugar, and the proper use of these came back into balance.

When I could no longer comfort myself with food, I ran to God for comfort. I recovered all the lost thought time and productivity I had lent to my obsession with food and preoccupation with weight. All the hours of research and study were redirected. I had been relieved of the relentless burden of worry and fear over what I weighed. I felt the lightness of a captive who has been set free from a hard and unforgiving taskmaster. Before God set me free, all my efforts were never good enough, and I could never be thin enough.

My emotions tipped back into balance. They were no longer tied to the fragile, fickle red arrow of my scale. I hated myself when I was fat and loved myself when I was thin. My whole self-image could be shattered with the slight of a scale. The opinions or reactions of others to my physical shape had once dictated my sense of worth. Even when I was thin, I was tormented by fear. The obsession caused me to live on the edge of extreme elation or deep depression. I was at the mercy of the scale and public opinion.

Even on a natural fast you will experience an increase in clarity of eyesight. On a spiritual fast, your eyes will be stripped of any scales that have blinded them.

Fasting changed my perception by changing my focus. This, in turn, caused me to change the way I lived. I no longer lived for food or for what I weighed. I lived for God.

After the fast I saw everything differently. My eyes were

illuminated by God's Word and truth. I could see the right path, as well as my former errors in judgment. Fasting provided a new vision and direction for life. My eyes shifted away from *me* and toward my Father God.

Like David, I had *humbled myself with fasting*. (Read Psalm 35:13.) Whenever we humble ourselves, we bring ourselves into submission, or become subject. I brought my soul—and inevitably my body—under subjection to God's Word and truth. Before that, I had been in submission to the cravings and appetites of my flesh and soul.

> I proclaimed a fast, so that we might humble ourselves before our God and ask him for a safe journey for us and our children, with all our possessions.
>
> —Ezra 8:21

I was embarking on a journey. I was changing seasons in my life. I was leaving my life as a single woman to join my life to my husband's. I was leaving my home state and embarking into the unknown. It would mean children and travel. I wanted God's provision in every area of my life. I was humbled by my inability and called out for God's.

Fasting positions us to acknowledge God's provision in our lives. It communicates that He alone is our Source. We deny ourselves food and tell Him, "I only want You and what You provide."

When we lay aside the daily routine of food and drink or pleasures and leisure, we are able to reevaluate our priorities.

Here are a few of the benefits of fasting:

1. *Creates a new hunger.*

2. *Increased sensitivity* (Luke 2:36–38).

3. *Humility* (Ps. 35:13).

4. *Chastens or disciplines* (Ps. 69:10).

134

5. *Changes your appetite.*

6. *Increases your capacity.*

7. *Answered prayer* (Isa. 58:9).

8. *Protection and provision* (Isa. 58:8).

9. *Looses chains of injustice* (Isa. 58:6).

10. *Frees the oppressed* (Isa. 58:6).

11. *Breaks every yoke* (Isa. 58:6).

12. *Food for the needy* (Isa. 58:7).

13. *Quick healing* (Isa. 58:8).

HUNGRY FOR MORE OF GOD

IF WE ARE NOT HUNGRY for God, it is because we have allowed our souls to be satisfied by other things. One morning when I was praying, I sensed the need for more of a hunger for God. I asked God to impart this hunger for Him within me. As I recorded my prayers in my journal, I waited for a response from God.

As quickly as I could write, He answered me. He showed me that I was the one responsible for my diminished hunger level. He told me that if I wasn't hungry, it was because I was already full—filled with the cares, pleasures, and distractions of this world.

He told me that if I wanted to hunger spiritually in the midst of the abundance of things, I would need to fast. He revealed that I would need to fast the things that would distract, comfort, or distress me. I was nursing my fourth son at the time and knew that God would not call me to fast food. Instead, I realized that He was calling me to fast other things that pulled me from His presence.

So for a period of time I fasted TV, magazines, telephone calls that were not business-related, and desserts. I rearranged my schedule to accommodate more prayer and Bible reading. I did this for about a month, and when the month was over, I discovered that I had lost my appetite for some of the things I had laid aside. I also sensed an increased discernment. I had previously been desensitized by the abundance of noise, voices, and other distractions.

Now it was easier to hear God's voice. The natural noise level in my house (with four young boys) had not varied; it was the noise level in my mind that had been reduced.

If we reserve fasting for only the times when we can physically leave or lock ourselves away, we will not fast very often.

As a mother I am experiencing a season when my children have legitimate demands on my time. God didn't tell me to check into a hotel room to fast for a few days. He probably knew that if He had told me that, I would just pass out and sleep the whole time. He wanted me to develop the ability to fast within the busy lifestyle that I live.

God wants to be an integral part of our lives every day, not just when we're on the mountain. I have had to develop a listening ear, one that can hear God's voice amid the din and noise of a full household. I have learned to listen while I take a shower, do the dishes, and sort the laundry.

This may shock you, but most of the time on my knees has been spent emptying my heart and repenting. Once this is done, I can usually hear God's voice whenever He desires to speak to me.

When I prepare for a service, I study and make pages of notes. Often I never use them. I do the notes for my sake, to put my mind at ease. The real preparation for the service comes when I confess and cleanse my heart before the Lord.

This allows the Holy Spirit to flow through me. It separates the precious and holy (God's Word and anointing) from the vile (my agenda or prejudices). I separate myself for whatever time it takes until I sense this process has taken place.

Separated Unto God

FASTING IS NOT just about food; it is about separation. This separation represents a consecration to the Lord, a change in our relationship with Him.

God posed this question to Israel:

> Is this the kind of fast I have chosen, only a day for a man to humble himself? Is it only for bowing one's head like a reed and for lying on sackcloth and ashes? Is that what you call a fast, a day acceptable to the LORD?
>
> —ISAIAH 58:5

The fast of the Israelites had been reduced to religious motions and the denial of food. The prophet Isaiah was saying that the Israelites had reduced fasting to a one-day ritual and lost the substance behind the fast. They had lost contact with God's heart on the matter.

God imparts His outlook on fasting by outlining the manner of fasting that truly pleases Him:

> Is not this the kind of fasting I have chosen: to loose the chains of injustice and untie the cords of the yoke, to set the oppressed free and break every yoke? Is it not to share your food with the hungry and to provide the poor wanderer with shelter—when you see the naked, to clothe him, and not to turn away from your own flesh and blood?
>
> —ISAIAH 58:6–7

God did not want a single day set aside now and then to occasionally honor Him. He wanted a radical and profound change of lifestyle. He did not want legalism; He wanted transformation. In the same manner, Jesus confronted the Pharisees with the observation that they tithed their garden herbs yet neglected the weightier things. The Pharisees were experts in the law but not in love. They turned away from the poor and from doing good.

God told His people that if they would reach out beyond themselves, then everything they had tried to get for themselves would be provided by Him. He promised:

> Then your light will break forth like the dawn, and your healing will quickly appear; then your righteousness will go before you, and the glory of the LORD will be your rear guard. Then you will call, and the LORD will answer; you will cry for help, and he will say: Here am I.
> —ISAIAH 58:8–9

God promised to bring His light to their darkness, to heal, and to make them righteous. He promised that His glory would guard them. He promised to answer their prayers and to help them in their time of need.

He repeats His outline of the conditions of His blessings and His vision for their lives:

> If you do away with the yoke of oppression, with the pointing finger and malicious talk, and if you spend yourselves on behalf of the hungry and satisfy the needs of the oppressed . . .
> —ISAIAH 58:9–10

God wants us to spend ourselves on the needs of others and to lift those who are oppressed. He wants the fast to be a turning point when we lay aside all accusation and judging. He wants the destruction of gossip and slander to be stopped. He wants our focus to shift from ourselves to others. God's focus is upon His children. When we selflessly love, we grasp God's heart. He reaffirms His promises with:

> . . . then your light will rise in the darkness, and your night will become like the noonday. The LORD will guide you always; he will satisfy your needs in a sun-scorched land and will strengthen your frame. You will be like a well-watered

garden, like a spring whose waters never fail.
—ISAIAH 58:10–11

Light will rise out of obscure darkness—so much light that your night will be as the noonday. You are assured by the promise of God's divine guidance that your needs will be met, though all that surrounds you is scorched. Any hardship God will use to strengthen your frame. You will be like a well-watered garden, fed by a spring that never fails. What more could you ask for? But the list of benefits does not end there. It continues:

> "Your people will rebuild the ancient ruins and will raise up the age-old foundations; you will be called Repairer of Broken Walls, Restorer of Streets with Dwellings. If you keep your feet from breaking the Sabbath and from doing as you please on my holy day, if you call the Sabbath a delight and the LORD's holy day honorable, and if you honor it by not going your own way and not doing as you please or speaking idle words, then you will find your joy in the LORD, and I will cause you to ride on the heights of the land and to feast on the inheritance of your father Jacob." The mouth of the LORD has spoken.
> —ISAIAH 58:12–14

None of these blessings are the provision of the earth; nor are they the provision of man. They are the blessings of God. They are His blessings in response to our change of heart.

God is challenging us to fast so that we might become women who are transformed. Whenever Israel truly fasted and turned to God for His assistance, He heard them. He responded with protection, provision, direction, and healing.

There is not one of us who, in our own strength, can provide all these blessings. No matter how much money or wisdom we have, we will always fail if we trust those things. God will never fail those of us who trust in Him.

He shares insight and secrets with those who fear before Him.

There was a widow woman named Anna, and she was very old:

> She never left the temple but worshiped night and day, fasting and praying. Coming up to them at that very moment, she gave thanks to God and spoke about the child to all who were looking forward to the redemption of Jerusalem.
>
> —LUKE 2:37–38

This very old woman who prayed and fasted could see better than the priest and the young people around her. She recognized that Jesus was the long-awaited Messiah when He was only eight days old. The Pharisees could not even recognize Him at thirty-three when He was casting out devils. Yet this elderly mother of the faith knew Jesus by the Spirit, as He was cradled in His mother's arms.

Anna was a true prophetess who encouraged those who were watching and waiting for Israel's redemption. Her prayers and fasting had given her prophetic insight.

You may or may not be in a position to fast food. Only *you* can answer that. But *everyone* is in a position to fast *something*. It may be TV, telephone, magazines, sports, shopping, or hobbies. All of us have areas in which we hide ourselves or waste our time.

I challenge you to go before our Father and ask Him by the power of the Holy Spirit to expose any areas that could be fasted. Read again the list of benefits for those who fast. Better yet, dig deeper. Because of limited space, I only included a sampling of scriptures. There are more.

Every believer should fast periodically. It is an act of separation to our Father. Jesus gave us invaluable insight on fasting:

> Moreover, when you fast, do not be like the hypocrites, with a sad countenance. For they disfigure their faces that they may appear to men to be fasting. Assuredly, I say to you, they have their reward.
>
> —MATTHEW 6:16, NKJV

TRUE AND FALSE FASTING

HYPOCRITE IS ANOTHER name for "impostor." An impostor is "one who deceives others by an assumed character or false pretenses." The hypocrite, or imposter, *pretends* to fast unto the Lord, when really it is for the accolades of man. The focus of such a fast is pious religious appearance, and the reward is the awe of man. These individuals will receive nothing from the hand of God. The hypocrite wants to be great among men. But we must choose between the reward of man and the reward of God. The religious fast is rewarded by man, while the fast of the broken and contrite is rewarded by God. Jesus continued:

> But you, when you fast, anoint your head and wash your face, so that you do not appear to men to be fasting, but to your Father who is in the secret place; and your Father who sees in secret will reward you openly.
> —MATTHEW 6:17–18, NKJV

Fasting is not a burden but a privilege. It is intimate and private. It originates in the secret place between you and God. He waits in that secret place for you to join Him. After you visit with Him in secret, He will reward you openly. Inward transformation brings about outward anointing, blessing, and provision. Inward transformation positions you for the promotion of the Lord. He will:

> Prepare a table before me in the presence of my enemies. You anoint my head with oil; my cup overflows. Surely goodness and love will follow me all the days of my life, and I will dwell in the house of the LORD forever.
> —PSALM 23:5–6

This describes the open reward of the Lord. It is a feast of provision and assurance of His presence. This is granted even in the midst of opposition.

*In the past, how have you viewed fasting?*_____

_____

_____

_____

_____

_____

*Have you been prone to diet?*_____

Have you ever fasted for a turning point or to receive answers? __

_____

While reading this chapter, did you feel a desire stirring within you to fast? _____

*If you did, I believe it is the Holy Spirit calling you to a deeper level in your walk with God. Write down some reasons or prayer requests for which you might fast.*_____

_____

_____

_____

_____

What are some areas in your life where you could apply the principle of fasting (for example—TV, magazines, phone, etc.)? _____

_____

_____

_____

_____

It is important that you stick with it when you make a commitment to God. It would be better to vow nothing than to pledge yourself casually. Allow for time to think and pray before committing yourself. Once you know what God has revealed for you, study the scriptures given on fasting in this chapter and reference others in your own private study. Take fasting seriously and let your respect and awe of God guard you as you walk into this new season of spiritual growth and insight.

We are

looking for something

we have never seen, yet we will

recognize it when we

see it.

11

"*I Found It!*"

A cord of three strands is not quickly broken.
                    —*ECCLESIASTES 4:12*

AS WE CLOSE the chapter on fasting we are at a pivotal point. We will turn aside from the dark path of what *is not* the measure of a woman and step toward the lighted path of God's true standard of measurement. Until now, we have searched here and there, looking for but not finding a complete answer. We have only glimpsed its foreshadow. With each new revelation, we have come closer to the answer we pursue.

Whenever we have lost an item, we will search in one place, then another. At first it might be discouraging when we don't find the misplaced item where we initially search. But each disappointment only narrows the options. We may say, "I've looked in the closet, my dresser, my purses, my coat pockets, and I still can't find it! It must be somewhere I had not thought to look." Then we quiet ourselves and for the first time stop our frantic and sometimes panicked search. We sit or kneel down and say, "God, I can't find what I am looking for. Holy Spirit, please quicken to my memory where it is."

"God Talked to Me!"

My second son, Austin, was four years old when we bought him some Legos that were all his own. Before this, most of his toys were his older brother's first, and he shared them. Or if he did receive Legos of his own, his older brother would quickly negotiate with him and talk him into combining them into one collection. On his birthday, we bought Austin a little Lego motorcycle police set that was his alone.

We sat him down and explained, "These are just for you. They aren't for Addison, and they are too grown up for Alexander. They're yours!"

Austin beamed as he carried the new Lego set off to a place of honor in the toy room.

Whenever anyone else tried to take the Legos, we'd remind, "Those are Austin's. You may only play with them if he has given you permission."

A month or so went by without any incident or loss. Then it happened. I was in the shower one morning when a frantic knock sounded at my door. Austin appeared, his face red and streaked with tears.

"Mom, I can't find my Lego guy!"

Austin's "Lego guy" was a policeman about two inches high that rode a plastic motorcycle. My oldest son was at school and Alexander was down for a nap. I could see that Austin was panicked, but I needed to finish my shower, so I made a suggestion.

"Go look on the dresser by your bed."

Austin's blond curls bounced as he whirled around and out the bathroom door. I could see that he was on a mission. I continued

146

to wash my hair, and prayed under my breath, "God, help Austin find his Lego guy. It means so much to him."

God immediately gave me an answer, though I had not expected one. (Yes, a lot of times this happens to me in the shower.)

"Tell him to kneel down and ask Me and I will show him where it is."

Moments later, Austin again burst into my bathroom.

"Mom, it's not there!" His little face reflected his desperation.

I thought for a moment, trying to suggest a more unusual place to find the toy.

"See if it fell into the silk tree under the loft. A lot of toys fall in. Shake its branches; I bet it's there," I confidently offered.

Immediately I sensed God's displeasure. I reasoned, *But God, Austin is a four-year-old! If I tell him You are going to talk to him and You don't, it will devastate him! He won't understand it.*

I could tell God wasn't convinced. So I bartered, *If he comes in again and hasn't found it, I'll tell him what You said.*

Secretly I began to rush my shower in the hope of getting out before Austin came in again. Then I could help him look. As I was drying off, the door flew open again. Austin was very discouraged and crying.

"It's lost, Mommy! I can't find it. Please come help me!"

I looked at his sweet, innocent, trusting face. He was confident that if only I helped him, he would find his Lego guy. I could be the hero . . . or I could repeat the Holy Spirit's words to me.

I lowered my voice to calm him, "Austin, while I was in the shower God told me that if you will go upstairs, kneel down, and ask Him where your Lego guy is, He will show you."

He calmed down and with a serious face turned and left for the loft. My heart flew into a panic: *What if He didn't! What if I hadn't heard from God and only imagined that I had! I'll have a bigger mess than a lost Lego man!* I began to pray again when the Holy Spirit questioned me, "Whose child is this?"

I was always saying that my children were not my own but God's; now this was where the rubber met the road.

"He's Yours," I answered.

A few moments later I heard jumping and shouting overhead, followed by rapid and heavy footsteps down the stairs. In a moment Austin was in my room, and clutched in his fist was his little Lego man! He was jumping up and down with joy and yelling, "God talked to me! God talked to me!"

Austin was oblivious to finding the lost toy, because he had heard from his Maker! We both hugged and jumped until he settled down. Wrapped in my towel, I knelt and asked, "Austin, tell me what happened."

"I went upstairs, knelt down, and asked God—and He told me my Lego guy was on top of the bookcase," Austin answered matter of factly. He seemed surprised that I would question him, since he had only followed my instructions.

Retrieval of a Lego guy from the top of the bookcase would involve my four-year-old son climbing up and standing on the arm of the sofa. The toy could only have arrived on top of the bookcase if thrown there by a brother or placed there by an adult. It was impossible for Austin to reach that height without climbing.

"How did you hear God? What did He say?" I probed.

He cocked his head, and replied, "He talked to me in my head and said, 'It is on the bookshelf.'" Then the whole concept of God talking to him overwhelmed him again, and Austin began hopping and chanting, "God talked to me! God talked to me!"

Whenever he looks for something and cannot find it, I always remind him of this incident and Austin will go off to pray. It is usually just a matter of time before the lost item is retrieved. It is yet another chance for my son to acknowledge God's guidance in his life.

A THREEFOLD CORD

WE ARE NOT looking for a mere object but for a blending of truth. We are looking for something we have never seen, yet we will recognize it when we see it. I believe the true measure of a woman is a threefold cord.

A cord of three strands is not quickly broken.
—ECCLESIASTES 4:12

This triune cord represents an intricate and intertwined balance in the value or measure of an individual. The number "three" is repeated frequently throughout the Bible as a divine representation of balance. We have already learned that the first thread in our cord is *our faith in God*. Before we go on to the second thread, I would like for us to pray and again acknowledge God's hand in our search:

Father, please show me the true measure of a woman . . . of myself. I've looked in many places and have not found it there. I looked in the past, but it was filled with pain and joys that had already faded. I looked at the possessions that surround me, but they are lifeless and cannot answer me. I asked my friends and family, but they too were searching. I did not find it in my profession or looks. They are what I do or what I look like, not what I am. I am not the measure of my marital status whether single, married, widowed, or divorced.

I hold a strand of faith and I believe that You are, and that You will reward my diligent search for truth. As I go further, give me eyes to see, ears to hear, and a heart to perceive and understand. Amen.

When I began to write this book, I was searching. *I knew I was not* the measure of a woman. *I knew what was not* the measure of a woman. But I was uncertain and hesitant about what that true measure actually was.

God assured me that if I would write, He would show me. I agreed and trusted God for His answers. He began by expanding my list of what that measure was not. Below is a brief list. Though it is not exhaustive, these were the things that most pertained to me. Some are obvious; others are not.

You are not—

- *What you do*—wife, mother, career

- *Who you know*—friends, associations

- *What you know*—education and intelligence

- *What you've done*—accomplishments, your past

- *What you wear*—hair, clothing, image, makeup

- *What you weigh*—body size and shape

- *What you own (have)*—possessions, home, cars

- *Where you've been*—travel and experience

- *Your marital status*—married, single, widowed, divorced

- *The color of your skin*—racial, cultural, ethnic

- *Your gender*—male or female

The true gospel is always simple and pure. It transcends culture, gender, income, age, and time. It is truth for everyone, the truth for whosoever will. It was true yesterday. It is true today. It will be true tomorrow. Only truths in this category can set you free, for others vary with age, health, income, lifestyle, and relationships.

God would never attach the true worth of an individual to anything so frivolous. He is altogether wise and perfect, so He anchors His measure of truth to an eternal scale and strikes a threefold balance. The second chord, we will discuss in this chapter; the third, in the next. Please read the following verses as though you had never read them before:

> If I speak in the tongues of men and of angels, but have not love, I am only a resounding gong or a clanging cymbal. If

I have the gift of prophecy and can fathom all mysteries and all knowledge, and if I have a faith that can move mountains, but have not love, I am nothing. If I give all I possess to the poor and surrender my body to the flames, but have not love, I gain nothing.

Love is patient, love is kind. It does not envy, it does not boast, it is not proud. It is not rude, it is not self-seeking, it is not easily angered, it keeps no record of wrongs. Love does not delight in evil but rejoices with the truth. It always protects, always trusts, always hopes, always perseveres.

Love never fails. But where there are prophecies, they will cease; where there are tongues, they will be stilled; where there is knowledge, it will pass away. For we know in part and we prophesy in part, but when perfection comes, the imperfect disappears. When I was a child, I talked like a child, I thought like a child, I reasoned like a child. When I became a man, I put childish ways behind me. Now we see but a poor reflection as in a mirror; then we shall see face to face. Now I know in part; then I shall know fully, even as I am fully known.

And now these three remain: faith, hope and love. But the greatest of these is love.

—1 Corinthians 13:1–13

THE SECOND STRAND

THE SECOND MEASURE of a woman is *her love for God.* Scan the above scripture text again and notice there is no mention of the love between a man and a woman, nor of parents for their children. These are not mentioned because the love represented in this scripture supersedes the natural love of family. *We are not measured by how we are loved by others but by how much we love.*

The love described here is God's love shed abroad in our hearts. It is the love that encourages us to look closer into that dim and poor reflection and fall in love with Christ in us, the hope of glory.

151

Our reflection is clouded and distorted by our own visage, but the day will come when we will stand *face-to-face* and *know fully* as we are *fully known*. Our love for God will exceed our love of man and our love of self.

Paul begins by describing spiritual gifts and miraculous feats of faith. Then he describes great personal sacrifice to the point of death. He surmises that without love, all of these are as nothing. They have no value. Gifts, knowledge, faith, works, and sacrifice are all worthless without love.

Paul then describes the attributes and characteristics of love. The list of patience, kindness, humility, selflessness, and tolerance seems pale in comparison with the incredible feats described above. Then by the Spirit, he makes this proclamation: *Love never fails.*

All else passes away but love endures. Love is eternal. God's love for us never perishes, never varies, never falters, never ceases. Because it is never-ending, it is incorruptible. The capacity for this love is in each of us, for we are commanded to:

> "Love the Lord your God with all your heart and with all your soul and with all your mind." This is the first and greatest commandment. And the second is like it: "Love your neighbor as yourself." All the Law and the Prophets hang on these two commandments.
>
> —MATTHEW 22:37-40

God does not require us to do things that are possible. He requires us to do things that are *impossible* apart from Him. His commandments are only two and are listed in order of their pre-eminence. First, we are to love God with *all* our heart, soul, mind, and strength. After we have spent ourselves entirely in this pursuit, then we will be empowered to love our neighbor as ourselves.

For so long we have had it backward. We have tried to love ourselves so we could love our neighbors. We have tried to love our neighbors when we didn't love ourselves. But God is calling us to love Him so we can love our neighbors and ourselves.

If we spend ourselves on loving ourselves, *we* will become the focus. *Self-love* is always a work of the flesh and an exercise in frustration and futility. We will always find fault in ourselves. We will find iniquity, disappointment, and imperfection in ourselves. We can study our past and study ourselves and still not find any true answers.

If we spend ourselves trying to love others, they will become our focus. We will soon see their flaws and imperfections. People will fail and disappoint us. They will break their promises and reject and betray us. Even if all relationships remain perfect, we can love our husbands and our children and still not love God.

God wants us to love Him.

> Knowledge puffs up, but love builds up. The man who thinks he knows something does not yet know as he ought to know. But the man who loves God is known by God.
> —1 CORINTHIANS 8:1–3

Let's pull that phrase out and say it so you will hear it:

The woman who loves God is known by God.

It is of utmost importance that God knows us. Without this recognition, we cannot enter into His kingdom. There are a lot of references in the New Testament where individuals are told, "Depart! I don't know you." They knew *Him,* but He did not know *them.* By loving God, we are transformed into the image of His Son and therefore recognized as His children. Every father can recognize His own. He sees in their form and features the shadow of His own. God knows we can't even love Him without His help, so He has supplied a selfless love for us:

> Dear friends, let us love one another, for love comes from God. Everyone who loves has been born of God and knows God.
> —1 JOHN 4:7

153

Love comes from God, not from feelings, relationships, or from our circumstances. It is a divine impartation from our Father. . . .

> We love because he first loved us.
>
> —1 John 4:19

We can love Him because it is safe to do so. We will not be rejected. His love will not cease or change. It is limitless. When we look deep into the glass, we see an ever-increasing revelation of that love. The love of God frees us from fear.

> There is no fear in love. But perfect love drives out fear, because fear has to do with punishment. The one who fears is not made perfect in love.
>
> —1 John 4:18

If you are afraid, it is because you are trying to love others without first experiencing a love for God. You will always fail and fall short if you first attempt the love of others when you have not wholeheartedly pursued the love of God. In the love of God, you will find His gracious forgiveness so you can, in turn, forgive graciously. You find His love and therefore you can love.

Remember when you first got saved? You loved God so much because He had forgiven you of so much. It was easy to love others without even trying because you were so overwhelmed by the love of God.

We have no less need of His mercy now than we did then. In fact, we should love Him more because we know Him more.

But often we get our eyes off God and back onto ourselves or onto our brothers and sisters. Our vision becomes dim and our love waxes cold. We focus on our failures at loving instead of on the source of love. Now is the time to return our love to Him. We've made the mistake of trying to love others to prove our love for Him. We need to ask Him to renew our love for Him. We need to ask Him:

Place me like a seal over your heart, like a seal on your arm;
for love is as strong as death, . . . It burns like blazing fire,
like a mighty flame.
—SONG OF SOLOMON 8:6

We have been like wayward wives who loved others and forgot
our first true love. We lavished our works, affections, and
strength on the "husband" of religion and forgot the love of our
youth. Some no longer sense His love, but He has promised:

"In a surge of anger I hid my face from you for a moment,
but with everlasting kindness I will have compassion on
you," says the LORD your Redeemer.
—ISAIAH 54:8

The first true measure of a woman is her faith in God. The
second is her love for God. His love is everlasting, regardless of
our faithlessness. It is one standard by which He measures us.
Before we go any further, let's ask God to reignite a fiery and
passionate love for Him.

Let's answer some questions:

*Do you find yourself busy trying to love without first receiving God's
love?* _____

*Have you attempted to love your neighbor before loving God with all
your heart, soul, might, and strength?* _____

*At the end of your day, do you recount failures and fear God's
rejection?* _____

Do you know the difference between a bride and a wife? _____

Are you more a wife or a bride in your relationship with God? ____

_____

Do you remember that first love and how it empowered you? ____

_____

Are you ready to return to its purity and simplicity? _____

Please pray with me:

> *Dearest Father, I ask that You would impart Your love to me. I love You because You first loved me. Overwhelm me afresh with the revelation of Your love, mercy, and forgiveness. Baptize me in the pureness and life of Your love. I turn with my heart back to my first love and deny and denounce all my other empty ones. Forgive my wayward unfaithfulness and draw me to Your side. Transform me by Your love until I reflect Your glorious image. Amen.*

*The noble woman has
learned the secret of a beauty that
radiates from within. Her inward purity works
an outward radiance. She allows her measure of
faith to develop both the love of God and the
fear of the Lord in her life.*

12

The Third Strand

"Many women do noble things, but you surpass them all." Charm is deceptive, and beauty is fleeting; but a woman who fears the LORD is to be praised. Give her the reward she has earned, and let her works bring her praise at the city gate.
—PROVERBS 31:29–31

T HE THIRD STRAND is reverent and worshipful *fear of the Lord.* In the last chapter, we discussed how God recognizes us by the imparted love we have for Him. In this chapter, we will examine the importance of holy fear. This essential ingredient is put into perspective in Proverbs 31:29–31:

> "Many women do noble things, but you surpass them all." Charm is deceptive, and beauty is fleeting; but a woman who fears the LORD is to be praised. Give her the reward she has earned, and let her works bring her praise at the city gate.

Again, this measure is available to "whosoever will." It is another one of God's measures that is equally accessible to everyone. It is not dependent on intelligence, talent, looks, ability, or age. It is not a function of learning, experience, knowledge, wealth, poverty, social status, profession, possessions, marital status, children, associations, location, size, height, weight, or skin or hair color. It surpasses our past failures and successes. It outranks any position of leadership and overpowers any anointing on our lives.

The woman who fears the Lord will be praised. Her reverent fear will earn her an eternal reward. Her works will bring her praise at the gate.

The fear of the Lord is the final thread that intertwines and knots all the other strands together. Before we dig deeper into what the fear of the Lord is, let's look closer at our example.

THE "PROVERBS WOMAN"

JUST WHO WAS THIS virtuous woman described in Proverbs 31? Most scholars agree that she is Bathsheba. I believe God purposely chose Bathsheba for a number of reasons. First, she was a woman with a past.

Bathsheba was summoned by King David after he had watched her bathe. It was never her intent to seduce David. He spied her from high on his roof, as she was completing her purification rite after her menstrual cycle.

> One evening David got up from his bed and walked around on the roof of the palace. From the roof he saw a woman bathing. The woman was very beautiful . . . (She had purified herself from her uncleanness.)
> —2 SAMUEL 11:2, 4

It is hard for us to imagine life in the culture of biblical times. Messengers arrived at Bathsheba's door and escorted her to the king. When someone was summoned by the king, there was no such thing as disobedience. David slept with Bathsheba, then sent her away. Alone, she felt the weight and guilt of her adultery. Weeks later, she awoke sick and tired and realized she was with child. Alone and afraid, she sent word of her pregnancy to the king.

David responded by trying to manipulate her husband, Uriah, into sleeping with Bathsheba to cover his guilt and to make Uriah think he had been the one to get his wife pregnant. But Uriah was loyal to the king and would not allow himself the pleasure of enjoying his wife and home when everyone else in David's army was in the thick of battle. So David arranged for Uriah's death.

Bathsheba was a woman who had known pain. Forget Hollywood's interpretation of the story. Second Samuel 11:26 clearly says, "When Uriah's wife heard that her husband was dead, she mourned for him." There is no record of Abigail mourning the death of her husband. Abigail was excited to be free and came immediately to David. But look closely at the description of Bathsheba's marriage to David:

> After the time of mourning was over, David had her brought
> to his house, and she became his wife and bore him a son.
> —2 SAMUEL 11:27

Bathsheba had endured many things. There is almost no record of her feelings in the matter. She became David's wife and bore him a child. But notice whom God was upset with:

> But the thing David had done displeased the LORD.
> —2 SAMUEL 11:27

There was no mention of Bathsheba's share in the guilt. Less than a year after the death of her first husband, Bathsheba's first-born son was struck ill and died by the hand of the Lord (2 Sam. 12:15). Imagine what life was like for her.

Bathsheba shared David with his other wives, ones who would certainly be jealous. As she walked the private corridors of the palace, I'm sure she was the object of gossip and scorn. Then her sole comfort—her precious child—was killed because of the sin of David.

With the death of this child, David went to comfort Bathsheba and she became pregnant with Solomon. From Solomon's birth forward, the Lord loved this child, and confirmed His love and acceptance of this tiny life through the mouth of the same prophet who'd spoken the word that smote Bathsheba's first son. In Solomon, God removed Bathsheba's reproach and the reproach of their marriage covenant. God was foreshadowing His love for and restoration of Bathsheba.

Bathsheba is an example to all women who have known pain, immorality, abuse, rejection, and slander. She rose above it all and remained true to her faith in, love for, and fear of God. Her response to all these injuries could have been very different.

She could have resented David—and God—for the death of her first son. She could have refused to forgive David. Through each hardship she allowed her faith, love, and holy fear to guide her response and set her course in life. How different from the royal wife, Michal, who in response to hardship had despised David. God blessed and honored Bathsheba's heart determination. *God caused the wisest king of men to declare her to be the noblest of all women.*

This is an example of the power of the gospel in which we trust. It transforms women with a past into virtuous women with a glorious future. It takes adulteresses and turns them into noble queens. The righteousness of Bathsheba outlived any former malignment of her name.

Nobility is not merely a function of birth. With all the present scandal surrounding nobility, we know this to be true. An individual can be born into the lineage of kings and yet remain a fool. One can be a prince without ever being princely.

Some definitions of the word *noble* are "aristocratic, worthy, virtuous, valorous, gentle, generous, extraordinary, admirable, dignified, remarkable," and more. The word bears the connotation not of birthright but of a righteous life. Nobility is available to king and peasant, rich and poor, male and female. It requires courage and a servant's heart.

Let's delve deeper into the character of this noblewoman, Bathsheba, by drawing on the Amplified Bible and its commentary:

> Many daughters have done . . . nobly, and well . . . but you excel them all.
> —PROVERBS 31:29, AMP

This comment exalts Bathsheba above all others who have done noble and well. Her nobility and godliness exceeded all her present peers and her predecessors. She was not a military leader or a public figure; she was a woman at home, a mother, a wife, and an instructor in righteousness. Through her godly private life, she rises above—

- *Miriam:* Prophetic praise leader (Exod. 15:20–21)
- *Deborah:* Leader and military adviser (Judg. 4:4–10)
- *Huldah:* Prophetess (2 Kings 22:14)
- *Ruth:* Woman of faithfulness (Ruth 1:16)
- *Hannah:* Ideal wife and mother (1 Sam. 1:20, 2:19)
- *The Shunammite:* Gracious hostess (2 Kings 4:8–10)
- *Queen Esther:* Who risked her life (Esth. 4:16)
- *Abigail:* Intelligent and beautiful (1 Sam. 25:3)
- *Queen of Sheba:* Royal and noble (1 Kings 10)

Many of us will never hold such positions of public influence. Yet nobility and valor are available to us in the privacy of our own homes. God elevates His daughters who have developed the fear of the Lord in their lives.

SEVEN VIRTUES

IN THE PROVERBS 31 description, Bathsheba's life exhibits all seven Christian virtues that are later found in 2 Peter 1:5–7:

- *Goodness*

- *Knowledge*

- *Self-control*

- *Perseverance*

- *Godliness*

- *Brotherly kindness*

- *Love*

Before I drew the parallel that this woman depicted by Solomon was Bathsheba, his mother, I used to read the description of this mysterious and perfect woman and think, *Well, I'd be perfect too if I had her lifestyle . . . maids and servants to help me . . . a husband with great influence . . . my own spending money to buy fields for invest-ment . . . clothes of fine linen and purple. If I had all this, I'd feel good about myself and I'd act noble, too!* I dismissed the whole premise of such virtue as unattainable and outdated.

But it wasn't Bathsheba's apparel or lifestyle that made her noble. It was her heart. Nobility is not a function of finances. To prove this point, let's look at another royal beauty. Her response to her beauty and fine provisions was quite different. We find her description in Ezekiel 16:9–14:

> I bathed you with water and washed the blood from you and put ointments on you. I clothed you with an embroidered dress and put leather sandals on you. I dressed you in fine linen and covered you with costly garments. I adorned you with jewelry: I put bracelets on your arms and a necklace around your neck, and I put a ring on your nose, earrings on your ears and a beautiful crown on your head. So you were adorned with gold and silver; your clothes were of fine linen and costly fabric and embroidered cloth. Your food was fine flour, honey and olive oil. You became very beautiful and rose to be a queen. And your fame spread among the

nations on account of your beauty, because the splendor I had given you made your beauty perfect, declares the Sovereign LORD.

She was beautiful and dressed in fine linen. She ate the finest food, like the Proverbs 31 woman. She was adorned with the finest jewelry. Like Bathsheba, her beauty alone elevated her to the position of queen. In addition to beauty, God cloaked her in royal splendor and made her beauty perfect.

But you trusted in your beauty and used your fame to become a prostitute. You lavished your favors on anyone who passed by and your beauty became his.
—EZEKIEL 16:15

Both started out with a cleansing bath. Both were seen naked. Both were later clothed in fine linen. Both were beautiful. Both were queens. Both dined on fine foods. Both had royal children. Both had noble husbands. Both were favored by God. But that is where their similarities ended.

The unfaithful wife trusts in her beauty (Ezek. 16:15), while the noble one trusts in the Lord (Prov. 31:30). Though her nakedness is covered, the faithless wife uncovers her nakedness again (Ezek. 16:36), while the noble wife remains covered and covers the rest of her household in scarlet (Prov. 31:21). The unfaithful wife takes the Lord's provision of food for her and her children and squanders it on idolatry and harlotry (Ezek. 16:20). The faithful wife wisely provides food for her household (Prov. 31:15), then she extends food to the poor and needy (Prov. 31:20).

The faithless wife slaughters and sacrifices her children for her own convenience and advantage (Ezek. 16:21). The noble wife faithfully instructs her children. Her children bless her, while the blood of the wicked woman's children accuses her. The wicked wife squanders the provision of her household in harlotry and riotous promiscuity (Ezek. 16:26, 34). The noble wife watches carefully after her household (Prov. 31:27) and invests wisely.

Her husband safely trusts her with everything, knowing she will always do him good (Prov. 31:11–12). There is no trust between the adulteress wife and her husband, only treachery.

The wicked, faithless wife has nothing to look forward to but inevitable and horrible judgment, so she lives for the moment (Ezek. 16:38–41). The noblewoman can laugh with joy at the days ahead of her. There is no fear, worry, or dread (Prov. 31:25). She is blessed in this life and eternally rewarded (Prov. 31:29–31).

Women who trust in their own beauty and use the provision of the Lord to seduce and entertain themselves will find that as their beauty fades with age, their former lovers will turn on them. All flesh eventually ages and corrupts. A prostitute's beauty is short-lived and hardens with age. The faithless woman lives for the moment because she lacks the restraining fear of the Lord.

God again describes His rejection of this attitude in Ezekiel 16:49–50:

> Now this was the sin of your sister Sodom: She and her daughters were arrogant, overfed and unconcerned; they did not help the poor and needy. They were haughty and did detestable things before me. Therefore I did away with them as you have seen.

The Sodomites were arrogant, overfed, and unconcerned. Their sins were pride, lasciviousness, and apathy. They ignored the poor and needy. This self-centered attitude caused them to live a detestable, haughty lifestyle. God did not judge the Sodomites merely for homosexuality; that was just a symptom of a much deeper heart condition. Their proud and wicked hearts led them astray into perversion. God saw the inner motives behind the perverse sexual lifestyle. They were consumed with their luxury and abundance, heaping on themselves and reveling in their own beauty and accomplishments. In this case, inward corruption brought outward destruction.

THE REAL SECRET OF BEAUTY

THE NOBLEWOMAN has learned the secret of a beauty that radiates from within. Her inward purity works an outward radiance. She allows her measure of faith to develop both the love of God and the fear of the Lord in her life.

In order for Bathsheba to train Solomon in the fear of the Lord, she would have first had to realize this fear in her own personal life. I am certain that experiencing the death of a child at God's hand would readily impart a revelation of the fear of God. This holy fear drew her closer to God, not away from Him in cowardice. Though in her time women were not trained in the Scriptures, Bathsheba became educated in the instruction and wisdom of the Lord. She committed herself to raising up a godly son to one day sit on David's throne.

Time and again we hear Bathsheba's wisdom echoed in the words of Solomon. He described her as, "She speaks with wisdom, and faithful instruction is on her tongue" (Prov. 31:26). She imparted a constant practical application in the fear of the Lord for Solomon. She encouraged him to search for it.

> My son, if you accept my words and store up my commands within you, turning your ear to wisdom and applying your heart to understanding, and if you call out for insight and cry aloud for understanding, and if you look for it as for silver and search for it as for hidden treasure, then you will understand the fear of the LORD and find the knowledge of God. For the LORD gives wisdom, and from his mouth come knowledge and understanding.
>
> —PROVERBS 2:1–6

Wisdom was so ingrained in him that Solomon knew what he wanted before God even asked him. His parents had burned a desire for wisdom and the fear of the Lord into the very fiber of his being. He bore the heartfelt desire of his parents to know God's wisdom and to understand His holy fear. He knew of the brother who had come before him. He'd heard that the Lord loved him and had set him apart as a prince among princes. He knew that only wisdom could preserve and guide his life as king.

WISDOM ABOVE ALL ELSE

SOLOMON PURSUED wisdom all his life. As wise as he was, he still strayed by disobeying God's command concerning his foreign wives. They pulled his heart away from following the Lord and he strayed from following God with his whole heart.

After a prosperous forty-year reign, Solomon looked back on his life and gave this summation of his entire search:

> Now all has been heard; here is the conclusion of the matter:
> Fear God and keep his commandments, for this is the whole
> duty of man. For God will bring every deed into judgment,
> including every hidden thing, whether it is good or evil.
> —ECCLESIASTES 12:13–14

At the end of his life, he returns to the wisdom of his parents. He exhorts those who read his words to first fear God and secondly, to keep His commandments. Why? Because the day will come when each of us must stand before the greatest King and watch as He brings our every word and deed into judgment. Solomon was at the threshold of that judgment and could sense the urgency of what truly merited his time and attention.

As the wisest of all, he knew what was truly valuable. He perceived the scale of God's eternal and true measure. God is the ultimate judge of the true measure of a woman. He is only interested in what remains after the fire of truth purges all the chaff and dross.

Our sexual, sensual, cultural measures of a woman will be consumed before His holiness. Our self-righteous religious images will crumble under the pressure of His judgment. Our works of the flesh and meaningless activities will appear futile in the light of eternal purpose. How can we endure such judgment?

We cannot. So God covers us.

THE FUNCTION OF THE THREEFOLD CORD

THE MEASURE OF FAITH will cause us to believe that God is just and that He is good. We will embrace the gospel and hide ourselves in Christ. This grants us His righteousness. We will place no trust in ourselves or in our own righteousness. Denying ourselves, we will embrace the cross.

The measure of love will draw us closer to God. As we behold Him, we will be transformed by His image into His likeness.

The fear of God will keep us from returning to the path of destruction. It guards us and cleanses us from impurity. Holy fear imparts a saving knowledge of the Lord. It is the light that draws us nearer, while His love assures us and His faith empowers us.

The three strands of faith, love, and holy fear—when woven and braided firmly together—provide a safe and sure hold for us. They are the criteria by which God judges the motivations of our hearts. This standard is not limited merely to women but is applied to all who embrace the cross.

Knowing the fear of the Lord, what manner of women should we be? We must be noble ones, for we are destined for a royal lineage and priesthood. We must strip ourselves from the garments of the world, lay them aside, and pick up the pure garments of linen already provided for us.

The faithless woman was washed from her sin and shame only to return and revel in it. God has given each of us a new start, a royal lineage by way of marriage to Him. It no longer matters how we are measured by the world or the law, for a new and living way has been set before us. Walking in it means leaving behind the old and taking up the new. The old way of measuring ourselves must be buried. You cannot mix the old with the new, for God calls this mixture adultery. One standard of measure has been exchanged for another.

In what areas have you used the old, or world's, standard of measure-ment? (Please list.) _____

_____

_____

_____

How often do you revisit your past in your thought processes? _____

_____

Do the fears of the past overshadow your fear of the Lord? _____

_____

Do you understand the urgency and necessity for the fear of the Lord?

_____

What areas in your life need the application of these eternal standards?

_____

_____

Are you ready to apply that new standard to your life? _____

If so, pray with me:

> *Father God, forgive my unfaithfulness and for allowing the cor-ruption of the world to determine my relationship with You. I renounce all false and unjust weights and measures. Lord, I want to see clearly through Your standards and from Your per-spective. As I draw near, open my eyes that I might focus on Your reflection and be transformed in the revelation of its glory. Impart nobility into my life through faith in God, the love of God, and the fear of the Lord. I cry out for Your wisdom and counsel. Let me know Your holy ways. Implant in me the true measure of a woman that I might stand before You in confidence on that day when all is seen for what it really is. Let truth and purity be found in my inward parts that I might see You. Amen.*

Epilogue

I WRITE WITH an urgency in my spirit. The time will come, whether it is near or far, when each of us must individually stand before the holy God of the universe. It is imperative that we change our perspective from a temporal one to an eternal one.

This will not be easily accomplished, as there is an aggressive onslaught against this wisdom of eternity. The spirit of this world has lulled many of us into a false sense of security and comfort. It has encouraged us to compare ourselves with each other and with the world. But the standard by which we will be measured will not include these factors.

Our standard is our Master and Lord, Jesus Christ. It is one of unattainable holiness only found in those who are hid in Christ. Pursue Him, for He alone bears the image that radiates God's glory. Behold Him, and you will be changed and transformed by the power of the Holy Spirit into His likeness. This visage blends faith, love, and holy fear. It opens blind eyes and deaf ears. It transforms hearts of stone into tender hearts of flesh. If you want to know this Lord and Savior from the depths of your being, pray this prayer. I caution you—do not pray this prayer until you are ready to lay down your own life and take up His.

Dearest Father God, You are so holy, I cannot even look upon You, let alone approach You. In Your wisdom and mercy, You provided a perfect sacrifice, one that would cover the very deepest and darkest hidden sin in my life. You gave Your only Son in sacrifice that I might live. Though I am unworthy of this, Your love for me superseded my judgment. I lay my own life at Your feet and repent of my former life of sin and selfishness. Jesus, I embrace the cross and lay down my will that I might fulfill Yours. Wash me and I will be clean before You. I make You Lord of my life and Savior of my soul. I leave behind the kingdom of darkness as I now enter Your kingdom of light. Amen.

Other Books by John and Lisa Bevere:

The Fear of the Lord
Discover the Key to Intimately Knowing God

Friendship with the Lord
is reserved for those who fear Him.
—Psalm 25:14, NKJV

More than ever, there's something missing in our churches, our prayers, and in our personal lives. It's what builds intimacy into our relationship with God. It's what makes our lives real and pure. It's what transforms us into truly Spirit-led children of God. It is the fear of the Lord.

In this riveting book, author John Bevere exposes our need to fear God. With his lovingly confrontational style, he challenges us to reverence God anew in our worship and daily lives. He shows how the fear of the Lord is the key to knowing God as He yearns to be known, and that any other approach will inevitably result in judgment.

This profound message will provoke you to honor God in a way that will revolutionize your life.

"I cannot overemphasize the importance of this message. It is a book that should be read by every believer."

—John Bevere

VICTORY IN THE WILDERNESS *by John Bevere*
God, Where Are You?

Is this the cry of your heart? Does it seem your spiritual progress in the Lord has come to a halt—or even regressed? You wonder if you have missed God or somehow displeased Him, but that is not the case . . . you've just arrived at the wilderness! Now, don't misunderstand the purpose of the wilderness. It is not God's rejection, but the season of His preparation in your life. God intends for you to have *Victory in the Wilderness.*

Understanding this season is crucial to the successful completion of your journey. It is the road traveled by patriarchs and prophets in preparation for a fresh move of God.

Some issues addressed in this book:
- How God refines
- Is the wilderness necessary?
- Pressing through dry times
- What is the focus of the true prophetic?
- Why *where you are* is vital to *where you're going*

THE VOICE OF ONE CRYING *by John Bevere*
A Prophetic Message for Today!

God is restoring the prophetic to turn the hearts of His people to Him. Yet often this office is reduced to merely one who predicts the future by a word of knowledge or wisdom . . . rather than a declaration of the church's true condition and destiny. Many, fed up with hype and superficial ministry, are ready to receive the true prophetic message.

Some issues addressed in this book:
- Genuine vs. counterfeit conversion
- Message of the true prophetic
- Recognizing false prophets
- The Elijah anointing
- Idolatry in America
- Exposing deception

BREAKING INTIMIDATION *by John Bevere*

How to Overcome Fear and Release the Gift of God in Your Life

Countless Christians battle intimidation. Yet they wrestle with the side effects rather than the source. Intimidation is rooted in the fear of man. Proverbs 29:25 says, "The fear of man brings a snare . . ." This snare limits us so we don't reach our full potential.

Paul admonished Timothy, "The gift of God in you is dormant because you're intimidated!" (2 Tim. 1:6–7, paraphrased). An intimidated believer loses his position of spiritual authority. Without this authority his gifting from God remains dormant.

The Bible is filled with examples of God's people facing intimidation. Some overcame while others were overcome. This book is an in-depth look at these ancient references and present-day scenarios. The goal: to expose intimidation, break its fearful grip, and release God's gift and dominion in your life.

This is an urgent message for every child of God who desires to reach their full potential in their walk with Christ. Don't allow fear to hold you back!

OUT OF CONTROL AND LOVING IT! *by Lisa Bevere*

Is your life a whirlwind of turmoil? Are you hating it? It is because you are in control! In this candid and honest book, Lisa challenges you to relinquish control of your life to God. Are you tired of pretending to be free only to remain

captive? This book contains in-depth insight into how fear causes us to hold on when we should let go! Are you holding on? Abandon yourself to God's care!

- ■ Escaping captivity
- ■ Overcoming anger
- ■ Your past is not your future
- ■ Conquering fear
- ■ The strongholds of gossip
- ■ Self neglect vs. self denial

"This is one of the most powerful books I have read on the subject on control."
—*Marilyn Hickey, Marilyn Hickey Ministries*

"Next to the Bible, this book is perhaps the most important book a woman will ever read . . ." —*Lindsay Roberts, Oral Roberts Ministries*

Endorsed by additional women leaders:
Sharon Daugherty, Suzanne Hinn, Dr. Fuschia Pickett, Mary Brown, Gina Pearson, Cheryl Salem, and Paula White.

THE BAIT OF SATAN *by John Bevere*
Your Response Determines Your Future

This book exposes one of the most deceptive snares Satan uses to get believers out of the will of God. It is the trap of offense.

Most who are ensnared do not even realize it. But everyone must be made aware of this trap, because Jesus said, "It is impossible that offenses will not come" (Luke 17:1). The question is not, "Will you encounter the bait of Satan?" Rather it is, "How will you respond?" *Your response determines your future!* Don't let another person's sin or mistake affect your relationship with God!

"This book by my friend John Bevere is strong, strong, strong! I found new help from his fresh insights and uncompromising desire to help each of us recognize Satan's baits and avoid them at all costs."
—*Oral Roberts, Oral Roberts University*

THE DEVIL'S DOOR *by John Bevere*

In *The Bait of Satan,* John Bevere exposed the devil's number-one trap for believers today. In *The Devil's Door,* he reveals the easiest way the enemy gains access in the lives of Christians—through rebellion. Satan cleverly deceives believers into thinking that submission is bondage and that rebellion is freedom. This revealing book exposes the devil's deception, blocks his entrance into your life, and helps you enjoy God's blessing and protection.

■ This book contains challenging and life-changing truths.
■ What is the source of true kingdom authority?
■ Learn to shut this door and lock it!

Audio/Visual Messages:

By John and Lisa Bevere

Videos
"The Bait of Satan"
"The Baptism of Fire"
"Breaking Intimidation"
"Does God Know You?"
"Don't Faint Before Your Harvest"
"The Fear of the Lord"
"Passion for His Presence"
"You Asked For It"

Audiocassette Series (3 tapes)
"Armed to Suffer"
"By Order of the King"
"The Fear of the Lord"
"Pursue the High Call"
"Standing Strong in a World of Compromise"
"The Training Ground of Champions"
"Walking With God"
"Out of Control and Loving It!" (Lisa Bevere)

To order call 1-800-648-1477 (U.S. only)
or 407-889-9617

PLEASE CONTACT JOHN BEVERE MINISTRIES:
■ To receive JBM's free newsletter, *The Messenger*
■ To receive a free and complete color catalog
■ To inquire about inviting the ministry of
John and Lisa Bevere to your organization

JOHN BEVERE MINISTRIES
P. O. Box 2002, Apopka, FL 32704-2002 U.S.A.
Tel: 407-889-9617; Fax: 407-889-2065

About the Author

LISA TOSCANO BEVERE is the author of one of CBA's (Christian Booksellers Association) most popular books for women, *Out of Control and Loving It!* A dynamic speaker for retreats and women's conferences, Lisa is also a frequent guest on radio and television broadcasts.

In her books, *Out of Control and Loving It!* and *The True Measure of a Woman*, Lisa takes her readers on a journey through her own life in which she battled cancer, survived an eating disorder, and overcame some tumultuous relationships. These books have proven instrumental in liberating the lives of men and women alike. Lisa's writing style is candid, bold, and inspiring.

As a speaker, Lisa's unique ability to communicate straight from the heart encourages her audiences to seek the heart of God through a lifestyle of true holiness.

Lisa makes her home in Florida with her husband, John, and their four sons.